THROUGH IT ALL

REFLECTIONS ON

MY LIFE,

MY FAMILY,

AND MY FAITH

CHRISTINE KING FARRIS

ATRIA PAPERBACK

NEW YORK   LONDON   TORONTO   SYDNEY

ATRIA PAPERBACK

A Division of Simon & Schuster, Inc.
1230 Avenue of the Americas
New York, NY 10020

First Atria Paperback edition January 2010

ATRIA PAPERBACK and colophon are trademarks of Simon & Schuster, Inc.

For information about special discounts for bulk purchases,
please contact Simon & Schuster Special Sales at
1-800-456-6798 or business@simonandschuster.com.

Designed by Jaime Putorti

Manufactured in the United States of America

10 9 8 7 6 5 4 3 2

The Library of Congress has cataloged the hardcover edition as follows:

Farris, Christine King.
    Through it all : reflections on my life, my family, and my faith /
Christine King Farris.—1st Atria Books hardcover ed.
        p.   cm.
    1. Farris, Christine King.   2. African American women—Georgia—Atlanta—
Biography.   3. African American women educators—Georgia—Atlanta—
Biography.   4. King, Martin Luther, Jr., 1929–1968.   5. King family.
6. Civil rights movements—United States—History.   I. Title.
E185.97.F374A3   2009
323.092'2—dc22   2008045430

ISBN 978-1-4165-4881-2
ISBN 978-1-4165-4882-9 (pbk)
ISBN 978-1-4391-5511-0 (ebook)

This memoir is dedicated to the memory of my beloved parents, Martin Luther King, Sr., and Alberta Christine Williams King, and my brothers, Martin Luther King, Jr., and Alfred Daniel Williams King. It is also dedicated to my loving support team, Isaac Newton Farris, Sr., my husband of forty-eight years; my children, Isaac Newton Farris, Jr., and Angela Christine Farris Watkins; and my granddaughter, Farris Christine Watkins, upon whom will fall the mantle to continue the legacy of her ancestors.

CONTENTS

SECTION THREE

A SEASON OF GRIEF AND LOSS

SECTION FOUR

WORKING THROUGH PAIN AND GRIEF AND
THE JOURNEY TO FORGIVENESS

CONTENTS

PREFACE

*H*aving been blessed to see the sunrise on the eightieth year of my life, I find myself more convinced than ever of the biblical admonition that "to everything there is a season."

I am now embarking on a season of reflection. It's a time to look back at the panorama of my life with a mixture of awe, gratitude, and a very real sense of wonderment.

It's a time to come to terms with the reality that joy and pain are simply opposite sides of the same coin.

God knows, I have seen my fair share of each.

I was, of course, blessed to have been born into an established, staunchly middle-class, God-fearing, politically influential family. We lived on what was, at the time, probably the premier African American street in the nation—"Sweet" Auburn Avenue.

I've lived to witness one of the cornerstones of our family, my own mother, murdered by a deranged gunman as she played the organ in our church during a Sunday morning service.

I've witnessed the hand of providence and a joining of "the man and the moment" as my younger brother Martin Luther King, Jr., (who will forever be "ML" to me) headed the revolutionary nonviolent movement that in the middle of the twentieth century and helped to transform America. His leadership of that movement inspired multiple peaceful uprisings worldwide. Oppressed people from across the globe came to understand that they could, indeed, "overcome."

But more than that, they came to see that they could, in fact, be the architects of their own liberation.

I've lived to see the world's recognition of my brother's labor culminate in his being awarded the Nobel Peace Prize. I have seen his bithday designated a national holiday—the first such honor to be afforded an African American.

And yet, the inevitable ebb and flow of history led Martin to oppose his own government as it recklessly waged an unjust and immoral war in Vietnam. I watched his understanding and analysis evolve as he concluded that the freedom struggle required confronting what he termed the giant evil triplets, "racism, militarism, and poverty."

I have come to know and depend on the presence of a just and generous God. A God who has shown me, time and time again, two things: His presence in joy and rejoicing, and that He never puts upon us more than we can bear.

I have arrived at this point in my life having had the advantage of a large, supportive, and loving family. Naturally, we've borne, shared, and experienced all the ups and downs that confront any American family.

But my particular story is unique.

And it's this story, with all its peaks and valleys and all its facets, that I seek to share with you on the pages that follow.

It is the story of a family that has been blessed by God to play a role in the struggle to help America deliver on its promise of freedom, justice, and equality for all it citizens—especially for those we know as "the least of these." I believe this to the core of my being.

This is my story.

Willie Christine King Farris
Fall 2008
Atlanta, Georgia

THE FORCES THAT SHAPED OUR LIVES: HOW WE CAME TO BE

To paraphrase an old saying, I believe that all human beings are the sum of their parts.

By that, I mean that a number of factors go into making us the adults that we become. Genealogy, how one is raised—"home-training," as it used to be called—life experience, exposure to the larger world, the opportunity to travel, the care, patience, and concern of loving parents, healthy interaction with peers and role models: All these things, and the forces of both nature and nurture, combine to bring forth the persons we ultimately become.

What follows in this section are stories of the family that produced me. I am convinced that, to a certain extent, genealogy and DNA combined to set the arc of my life, and the lives of my two siblings—at birth.

I understand why the calling to participate in the freedom struggle was literally "in our blood."

I'm clear about where the emphasis on the value of an education came from—and there's no doubt in my mind how I came to select a profession as a life-long educator.

It was simply "in the blood."

I understand clearly the role religion has played in my life, and in the lives of my brothers, ML and AD.

I understand how both ML and AD came to be ministers on the front lines of the battle for human and civil rights.

And on that point I am compelled to make a very specific observation.

The world knows ML as a civil rights leader, and certainly as the recipient of the Nobel Peace Prize.

But by the same token, I want the world to understand and appreciate that AD, our "baby brother," was a significant civil rights leader in his own right. He was always there to aid and assist Martin in any way that was required. He was with him in Memphis when he died. He and his family also suffered and sacrificed in the struggle. His home was bombed and his life was at risk, like the lives of everyone else who made the conscious decision to stand for freedom, justice, and change.

None of us evolve into the people we become by abstract reasoning. The chapters that follow describe the foundations, people, and experiences that created us and set us on the course of our lives.

THE WILLIAMS AND KING FAMILIES: FROM WHENCE I HAVE COME

God has given me many blessings, for which I am eternally grateful. It would be an understatement to observe that my life has been extraordinary. What appears on the following pages is the result of my having reached the vantage point of eighty years. It is my feeble effort both to take stock of my life and to share it with others, in the hope that my story might provide inspiration and, perhaps, speak to the need to stand tall through joy and pain, success and tragedy, and to find a way to "keep on keeping on."

Generations of my family who came before us tilled the soil and gave us their shoulders to stand on. We have tried to respond to the call of conscience and the will of God.

Every now and then, I have to chuckle as I realize there are people who actually believe ML just appeared. They think he simply happened, that he appeared fully formed, without context, ready to change the world. Take it from his big sister, that's simply not the case.

We are the products of a long line of activists and ministers.

We come from a family of incredible men and women who served as leaders in their time and place, long before ML was ever thought of.

My brother was an ordinary man, called by a God in whom he had abundant faith. He took on incredible challenges, and he rendered extraordinary service to his fellow man. At the outset, it is critical to recognize that many of the gifts with which the public later associated ML came from those in our family who preceded him, including my maternal great-grandfather, Willis Williams, who was a slave and a minister. Actually, he was an "exhorter," which is what "Negro" ministers were called during the era of slavery. He was from Penfield, a small town in Greene County, Georgia, about seventy miles east of Atlanta.

Penfield is famous for its cemeteries, and cemeteries have certainly figured prominently in my life. Among the notables buried in Penfield are Jesse Mercer, one of the founders of Mercer University, and General James Edward Oglethorpe, a founder of Oglethorpe University, which began originally in a Penfield church.

There is a lot about the background of Willis Williams that I do not know. I do know, however, that he was married to Lucrecia Williams, who was thirty years his junior.

Before the Civil War, Willis and Lucrecia attended Penfield's Shiloh Baptist Church. In a practice that was probably unusual for the time, Shiloh counted both slaves and whites as full members of its congregation. My great-grandfather was owned by William N. Williams, who was also a member of Shiloh.

Consider the irony of that sentence for a moment: concurrent Christian church membership and simultaneous slave ownership.

Interestingly enough, Willis and Lucrecia joined Shiloh in

1846, before his owner joined. The records show that my great-grandparents left the church after the Civil War.

The Williams family grew during the war. On January 2, 1863, one day after Abraham Lincoln signed the Emancipation Proclamation, a son, my grandfather Adam Daniel (AD), was born to Willis and Lucrecia. The early years of his life were spent with his parents on the Williams plantation. Although I didn't know much about her, Granddaddy Adam Daniel had a twin sister whose name was Eve. She died very early on. Following his father's death in 1874, Granddaddy AD left the plantation with his mother.

My grandfather was quite a man. He arrived in Atlanta at age thirteen and remained there for the rest of his life. I was only three and a half years old when he died of a heart attack in our home on Auburn Avenue. Because I was so young, my memories of him are vague and fleeting. But I'm told he was tall and quite handsome.

I actually recall the spring day on which he died. It was March 21, 1931. I was in the kitchen trying to help my grandmother prepare breakfast. Suddenly we heard a loud thump on the floor. She sent me to find out what had happened. I returned and announced, "Granddaddy is sleeping on the floor." Apoplexy was ruled the official cause of death. Today, it would simply be called a stroke.

Following in the family's

MY GRANDFATHER REVEREND A. D. WILLIAMS, THE SECOND MINISTER IN THE FABLED HISTORY OF EBENEZER BAPTIST CHURCH.

ministerial tradition, my grandfather A. D. Williams served as the second pastor of Atlanta's Ebenezer Baptist Church. His tenure lasted thirty-seven years, from March 14, 1894, until his death.

Ebenezer had been in existence for a mere eight years when he assumed the pastorate. At that point, the church had roughly fifteen members. In his first year of leadership, he managed to add over seventy-five new members. He also found a way to purchase land in downtown Atlanta, on McGruder Street, where he constructed a new church.

My grandfather had a powerful, billowing voice. He was a great speaker and a superb organizer. He believed not only that the church should be involved in the lives of its members, but that it should be equally politically active in the community.

In those days, Jim Crow laws reigned supreme. They were given official sanction and undergirded by the U.S. Supreme Court's 1896 decision in *Plessy* v. *Ferguson*. Its ruling established the noxious "separate but equal" doctrine and gave legal justification to racial segregation.

Following the *Plessy* decision, the state of Louisiana adopted a new constitution, which contained a "grandfather clause." This clause held that for a person to be qualified to vote, the prospective elector's grandfather must also have been legally qualified to vote. Obviously, less than a generation removed from slavery, and following in *Plessy*'s wake, this was a naked attempt by the state to disenfranchise newly freed blacks. It was clearly an attempt to roll back whatever gains were made following the Civil War during Reconstruction.

Naturally, other southern states soon followed and adopted their own versions of the "grandfather clause." Granddaddy Williams saw it as his duty and responsibility, as both pastor and community activist, to combat these laws, which sanctioned and codified the systemic mistreatment and oppression of those of God's children who happened to be black citizens of southern states.

In this horrible period in American history, his primary targets became segregation, disparities in public education, unfair wages, discriminatory employment practices, and the general campaign of terror so expertly employed by the Ku Klux Klan, among whose tactics were church and home arson, lynching, castration, murder, intimidation, and other forms of torture.

From its inception in 1866, a scant three years after Emancipation, the Klan's overriding purpose had been the harassment and attempted resubjugation of the newly freed blacks and their descendants. This was particularly true after these former slaves won the right to vote with the ratification of the Constitution's Fifteenth Amendment in 1870.

Today, most people are aware of the Klan's sordid past and its violent, racist nature. They probably do not know, however, the full scope of the organization's reach during the period of my grandfather's ministry. As he was publicly opposing and rallying resistance to the countless atrocities committed by the Klan, some estimates peg the Klan's membership at as many as two million.

The atmosphere and stifling restrictions growing out of the Klan's reign is practically incomprehensible today. It was quite real and extraordinarily tangible in those days. The dignity of grown men crushed at the whim of these cowardly men in hoods. Their devious acts usually took place under the cover of darkness. Fear and terror were rampant, widespread, and thoroughly ingrained in black communities across the South.

Against this backdrop, it is important to appreciate the extent to which Granddaddy's outrage, expressed at Ebenezer and in the community at large, was an act of courage and defiance. This was, after all, a time in which black men died for not clearing a path on the sidewalk fast enough to suit some passing white man. Likewise, it was a time when staring for what was perceived as "too long" at some "flower of white femininity" could result in death. Young Emmett Till's alleged whistling at a white woman in Money, Mississippi, comes to mind. Fortunately, my grandfather survived the Klan's grip.

A. D. Williams was a freedom fighter. He was an early president of Atlanta's NAACP chapter. It was in this capacity that he led a boycott against the now-defunct newspaper the *Georgian*, the city's major daily at the time, arising from the derogatory descriptions of blacks that routinely appeared on its pages. This kind of treatment by the press was quite common at the turn of the twentieth century. He knew Negro Atlantans were hard-working, God-fearing, taxpaying citizens who didn't deserve these slanderous characterizations.

You can imagine the editor's shock when Granddaddy Williams and his delegation appeared in his office, not seeking menial jobs but *demanding* a new policy toward African Americans. Shortly after the boycott ended, the paper crumbled financially. But not before it had denounced my grandfather and "his kind" for attempting to take the city from its law-abiding white citizens.

On another occasion, he led a protest that stopped a proposed municipal bond issue in its tracks. The city fathers had intentionally designed a proposal with no provision for the high school education of black children. His activism and leadership on the bond question was responsible for the establishment of Atlanta's first black high school; as a result, Booker T. Washington High School for Negroes opened its doors in 1924.

That same year, my grandfather joined with Reverend Frank Quarles, pastor of Friendship Baptist Church, and over two thousand other delegates and supporters in establishing the National Baptist Convention.

Planning and protest strategy meetings took place in numerous black churches, often lasting until well into the night. My grandfather, and Ebenezer, were at the forefront of many of these meetings, meetings that, in fact, laid the foundation for what some fifty years later would become known as the modern Civil Rights Era.

Granddad's wife, my maternal grandmother, was born Jennie Celeste Parks in April 1873. She was the daughter of William and Fannie Parks, both of whom were born in Georgia, in 1825 and 1830, respectively. She married Granddaddy on October 29, 1899. This was a departure from the prevailing southern religious tradition of the times; my grandfather had been single and the pastor of Ebenezer for over five years before they wed.

"Mama," as we called her, served as president of Ebenezer's Women's Missionary Society. She also helped organize various fund-raising drives and participated in other activities to serve the church and community. She assisted the needy with food, clothing, and shelter. She worked with other women in the church as they discussed how best to assist their husbands in working to improve the lives of others during this period of second-class citizenship and segregation.

I have often wondered how Mama was able to accomplish

My grandmother Jennie Celeste Parks Williams—a stylish and classy woman whom I always wanted to emulate when I grew up.

what she did. What motivated her and gave her strength? Having avoided being born into slavery by less than ten years, she could easily have fallen victim to the residual mentality of the times: timidity, a feeling of hopelessness, shattered dreams, and psychological trauma. Or she could easily have slipped by the wayside and led a simple, nondescript life.

Clearly, she chose not to. Her life was extraordinary. It was characterized by unselfishness and by an unwavering commitment to God and to the community. She always put the needs of others before her own.

Many women of her day worked in the home. They were expected to tend to their families, raise the children, cook, clean, sew, and make few waves. My grandmother was a bold exception to this formula. She had her own unique trajectory, one that was created and not dictated.

For example, education was a major factor in her life. For most blacks during this period, education was simply unattainable. Many were barely literate. Sheer survival was the objective of most of her contemporaries. There was a widespread perception that education was reserved for whites, and only on rare occasions, for a few select blacks.

Mama's inner drive and determination caused her to buck this trend. Her quest for an education led her to Spelman Seminary, which then, as now, was the pinnacle of educational excellence for African American women. My grandmother's admission to Spelman marked the beginning of a rich and proud tradition for the women of our family.

Her matriculation set an example of achievement and high standards for all the women of the King family who followed. In her own special, quiet way, she demonstrated to the community, and most important, to us, the realm of possibility and the capacity to dream.

Mama was also known for two other things: a love of cooking and her impeccable sense of style.

Cooking and the loving preparation of family meals were a big part of her life. Wonderful food was always plentiful, but never more so than on Sundays. I can remember the table overflowing with fresh greens from the garden, baked macaroni and cheese, fried chicken, glazed ham, smothered pork chops, and corn on the cob. Desserts included cakes and pies, bread pudding, and various cobblers.

As for her fashion sense, Mama kept it simple. She loved shoes, gloves, hats, and her black purse. She was understated and never chose anything outlandish. Whenever Mrs. A. D. Williams appeared in public, she was so elegant that Gordon Parks himself could have been preparing to photograph her for the latest issue of *Life* or *Jet* magazine. I remember as a little girl hiding near the screen door and watching her as she stepped onto the porch preparing to leave the house. She always wore wonderful fragrances and would stand regally waiting on my grandfather to pull the car up to whisk her away. I watched all this with fascination, silently praying that God would make me just like her when I grew up.

On Sunday, May 4, 1941, Mama had a speaking engagement at

Mount Olive Baptist Church in Atlanta. She was to deliver the keynote address for the Women's Day Service. While sitting on the pew awaiting her turn to speak, she slumped over. Mama died right there in church. We learned this tragic news as we returned home from our own regular service at Ebenezer.

We were all in shock, particularly ML, who, against my father's directions, had snuck downtown to see a parade. He believed Mama's death was God's way of punishing him for having disobeyed our father. Finally, Dad had to explain to him that death always occurred according to God's plan.

It took ML months to come to terms with Mama's loss. After this experience, more than one person observed that he seemed to have grown more mature.

Mama's sister, "Aunt Ida" Worthem, who lived with us, was devastated by her loss. Aunt Ida had always taken excellent care of us. She loved telling stories of the "old times" and reading to us, often directly from an encyclopedia. Right after Mama died, Aunt Ida seemed to lose the will to live. She barely ate and hardly talked anymore. She stayed confined to her room more often than not. Shortly after we lost Mama, Aunt Ida died as well. I miss them both, terribly, to this day.

James Albert King was my paternal grandfather. He was born in Ohio in December 1864. The King Papers Project has looked into his background. Unfortunately, not much information exists on the record. We do know that he was not a slave. More likely than not, he was an indentured servant of some sort.

My paternal grandmother was Delia Linsey. She was born in Henry County, Georgia, in 1875 to Jim Long and Jane Linsey.

My paternal grandparents married in Stockbridge, Georgia, on

August 20, 1895. They produced my father, Michael King (later to become Martin Luther King, Sr.), and nine other children: my aunts Woodie, Cleo, Lenora, Lucille, and Ruby, and my uncles James, Henry, and Joel. They had one son, Uncle Lucius, who died as an infant. Into this brood my father was born December 19, 1899.

Granddaddy King was a lean, tough man, who also was troubled. His problems led him to drink—occasionally at first, but eventually he progressed into full-fledged alcoholism. He worked in a Stockbridge rock quarry where he lost a portion of his right hand in an explosion. Unable to do quarry work after the explosion, he looked for full-time work as a sharecropper. As part of this lifestyle, the family moved quite often. This situation affected him and his family the rest of his life.

It was against this backdrop that Granddaddy King struggled to provide for his family as best he could. There were nights when, returning home after being marginalized and exploited all day, he would pick fights with his oldest son, my father. Some of these confrontations lasted until well into the night. He'd often fall asleep on the kitchen floor with a bottle inside his hat near his head. Incredibly, the mornings following these tirades were often filled with the jokes and laughter of a conflicted father trying to love and provide for his family. The family, in turn, naturally lived on edge. They knew nightfall was likely to bring more of the violence and the unknown to which they had grown accustomed.

The story of how my parents, Michael King and Alberta Christine Williams, came to meet is romantic and charming. As a young man, Daddy attended Atlanta's Bryant Preparatory School.

Following in her mother's footsteps, my mother was a boarding student at Spelman Seminary. Bryant Prep was a few blocks from

"MOTHER DEAR." MY MOTHER, MRS. ALBERTA CHRISTINE WILLIAMS KING. SHE IS THE FIRST IN A LONG LINE OF CHRISTINES IN OUR FAMILY: MOTHER; MYSELF, WILLIE CHRISTINE; MY DAUGHTER, ANGELA CHRISTINE; AND MY GRANDDAUGHTER, FARRIS CHRISTINE WATKINS.

the home my mother shared with her parents on Auburn Avenue. Having heard stories of Reverend Williams's beautiful, intelligent daughter, a member of one of the city's most respected families, Michael King made it his business to walk past the home on his way back and forth to class. He hoped to catch a glimpse of Alberta on the porch but he never did.

When Dad finally did see my mother, she was hobbling down Auburn Avenue on crutches after breaking her ankle. Although he got a glimpse of her, they didn't actually meet. His opportunity finally came when he saw her walking home from Ebenezer. That very evening, the first time they had spoken, he got up the nerve to formally ask if she would consider "courting." After much contemplation, he got his answer.

They began "keeping company" during the summer of 1920. The courtship lasted for six years. On Thanksgiving Day 1926 they were married in a ceremony at Ebenezer. Reverends James M. Nabrit, Peter James Bryant, and E. R. Carter officiated. Their marriage lasted for forty-eight years, until my mother's death. Into it, three children were born—me and my two siblings, ML and AD.

This truly is a classic picture. It's one of my favorite family portraits. Shown here are my parents, my grandmother, Jennie Celeste Parks Williams, and me, between my two brothers, AD on the left and ML on the right.

As I think back on my childhood, one of the things that's definitely different today is that so few families sit together at the dinner table. This is a shame and, I think, something of a tragedy. In our home sit-down dinners were not optional. They were *mandatory*. The dinner table seating arrangements were carved in stone and unchanging. Daddy sat at the head of the table—no exceptions. My mother sat to his left. Mama and Aunt Ida sat to his right. To Dad's right sat ML and AD, in that exact order . . . and me. At the opposite end of the table from Daddy sat Mother Dear.

These meals were filled with laughter and joy, good eating, and most important, lessons from Mother and Daddy that I still cherish. They reinforced in us that we were as good as anybody, and that the segregation we saw all about us was mandated by law, that it was not proper, nor was it in keeping with our social and religious beliefs.

They talked to us about the realities of the world that we inhabited in the 1930s and 1940s, a world in which there was a deeply ingrained system constructed to hold black people back and in "our place." It was a world in which our progress and achievement were frustrated and denied. They taught us that our existence in such a world was the residual result of our being descendants of African slaves. They went on to explain that it was the present-day, tangible consequence of the fact that our skin was darker than that of our white contemporaries.

It was a world, for example, in which we were not allowed in the downtown movie theaters or department stores. Similarly, Negroes didn't visit the Grant Park Cyclorama, the diorama depicting the Civil War Battle of Atlanta, which was, at most, a few miles from our house.

Daddy taught us how to speak out against hatred and bigotry, and how to stand up for what was right. He would tell us, "If you stand up for what you believe in, and what's just, God will always be on your side." It was this simple philosophy that sustained us, time and time again, through tough times, tough decisions, and tough circumstances.

My father was the type who taught through example. No pun intended, but he vigorously practiced what he preached. He was a profound influence on us and certainly on ML, for above all else, Daddy was a *man*.

Once, when Daddy and ML were together in his car, a police officer pulled Dad over and referred to him as "boy." It was not uncommon in those days for whites to consciously degrade grown men by calling them "boy," or to refer to adult women as "gal." Daddy was having none of it. He pointed directly to ML, seated next to him, and said to the policeman, "This is a boy. I am a man, and until you call me one I will not listen to you." I have never believed that it was just some kind of cosmic happenstance that years later, as ML undertook the campaign for economic justice, the signs worn by striking sanitation workers in Memphis defiantly proclaimed, "I AM A MAN."

On another occasion, a shoe salesperson told Daddy and ML that he could not serve them in the front of the store because they were black. Daddy promptly left and went to another store where they could indeed be served at the front.

Not everything that occurred at the dining room table was political. Other lessons were learned and shared, too. We learned to stand upright and not slump over in the presence of others. We were taught to look people directly in the eye when we spoke to them. We learned to dress properly and appropriately at all times. In terms of dress, I'm not sure I can ever recall a time when my father was not wearing a necktie. Even if he had his sleeves rolled up, he would still have on his tie.

Respect for our elders was a given. This was also reinforced at the dinner table. Use of the words "No, ma'am" and "Yes, sir" was integral in determining whether a young man or woman had received the proper upbringing, whether he or she had "good manners" and had been "raised right."

Another major topic for discussion, of course, was education. We would talk about our day at school and the night's homework assignment, right there at the dinner table. We did our homework and memory work. Math and English lessons had to be recited.

A CASUAL, UNEVENTFUL DAY. HERE I'M SHOWN SIMPLY RELAXING AND ENJOYING MY FAMILY, WITH MOM AND ML IN MY PARENTS' BACKYARD.

Grammar corrections were made; nobody got away with asking, "Where's that at?" Mother would quickly launch into a discussion of the proper use of prepositional phrases. These lessons stuck so well that, even in her absence, we took to correcting each other's use of the English language.

The lessons at the dinner table, the dialogue, and the food were all nourishing. We often had guests who contributed to the stimulating atmosphere and conversation as well.

Among our frequent visitors were Reverend Sandy Ray of Brooklyn's Cornerstone Baptist Church and Dr. Melvin Watson, whose father was the clerk at Ebenezer. Dr. Melvin Watson went on to earn his doctorate from Boston University and would later give me valuable encouragement and support as I prepared to attend Columbia University.

2

BIG SISTER CHRISTINE, ML, AND AD

*A*rriving earlier than expected, I came into the world in an upstairs bedroom at 501 Auburn Avenue on September 11, 1927. My full name is Willie Christine King. Hardly anyone knows my first name. I am rarely called by it. "Willie" was chosen as a way to pay homage to the Williams side of my family; it was given in tribute to my maternal grandfather, Reverend A. D. Williams.

My first act on earth, my arrival itself, created a bit of a dilemma for my parents. Because I was born somewhat earlier than expected, and because I was my parents' first child, they hadn't actually gotten around to buying a crib before I was born. This turned out to be a problem solved easily enough. My first few days were spent in a chifforobe drawer. (I'm sure there are readers who are unfamiliar with that term. A chifforobe is a piece of furniture, very much like a present-day chest of drawers.) My new lodging was only temporary. I "moved" to my own crib after just a couple of days.

Sixteen months later, my brother ML was born in the same room. The child who would be known to the world as Martin Luther King, Jr., started life as Michael King, Jr. There is, of course, a story behind this name change. My paternal grandfather, James Albert King, told my father that when he was born, he was named Martin after one uncle and Luther after another. Before Granddaddy King died, he made Daddy promise to get this name change confusion cleared up. True to his word, after Granddaddy King died my father did just that; he legally changed the names of himself and his oldest son.

ME IN MY MOTHER'S ARMS AS AN INFANT.

My younger brother, Alfred Daniel Williams King, was born July 30, 1930. He was partially named after Granddaddy Adam Daniel Williams. As was the common in those days, we immediately referred to him by his initials. Thus, he became universally known as AD. Like his older siblings, he was born in the family home. He also inherited the crib that ML had used before him.

Being both the eldest and a girl wasn't always easy, particularly when my two younger siblings were bullheaded boys, much more interested in leading than in following. Somehow, I managed to hold my own. As you would expect, I showed ML and AD who was really running the show every chance I got. I was never a prissy girl. On the contrary, anything my brothers did, I made it my business to do. I didn't want to be left out of all the fun. That's why I was often found out in the backyard playing hide and seek, football, stickball, dodge ball, and one of our favorites, "tag." I was pretty fast, if I say so myself, so I was above average at tag.

Being the big sister was not without its challenges. For example,

THIS PHOTO SHOWS A PLAYFUL SIDE OF ML. HERE HE'S SHOWN
HANGING FROM THE REAR WINDOW OF A CAR. HE'S WITH MOTHER
AND A GROUP OF EBENEZER MEMBERS.

like most girls, I liked playing with dolls, but in a household with two boys it was difficult keeping them to myself. My brothers liked to behead them and scatter their body parts throughout the house. You might find a leg in the bathroom, an arm upstairs in the hallway, or the head in the backyard in the weeds near the fence.

I'm happy to report that these days, I have quite a nice doll collection, due to folks' feeling sorry for me over the years and sending me dolls.

Despite being the baby, AD never acted it. From the start, he was the bravest and most "devilishly creative" of us all. He was also the ultimate prankster. Take, for example, the fox fur story.

Our grandmother—"Mama Jennie"—had an old fox fur, complete with head and glass eyes. We used to have a time frightening people with it. We'd duck out of sight behind shrubbery in the front yard and have a ball scaring unsuspecting folk as they walked by on the sidewalk. We'd tie the fox fur to a long stick and wait patiently for the next passersby to approach. When they got close enough, we'd wiggle and dangle the fox. It would be an understatement to say a great commotion followed. Women would scream and clutch their husbands by the arm. The men, for the sake of their wives or their own egos, would pretend not to be scared. It was a riot!

Our little prank went on for quite a while, but, when Daddy found out from one of the neighbors what we'd been up to, the jig was up. The game came to a screeching halt, as you would expect.

Daddy spoke to each of us individually, telling us never to do it again. ML and I had no intention of disobeying Daddy. That is, not until AD tried his best to convince us that we wouldn't be caught again. My bold and daring little brother did do it again. Luckily for him and for very specific parts of his anatomy, he didn't get caught. You see, nonviolence had not come into Daddy's home at that point.

BIG SISTER CHRISTINE WITH MY YOUNGER BROTHER ML, WHO CAME ALONG SIXTEEN MONTHS AFTER MY BIRTH.

AD was something else! I'll never forget an episode at Hanley's Funeral Home. A woman from church had died. At AD's urging, a group of us, me, the boys, Dolores Robinson, a lifelong playmate and girlfriend, and a few others went to Hanley's in an effort to see the body. The woman wasn't ready for viewing when we arrived. In those days, bodies were laid out on "cooling boards" before being placed in caskets. Somehow, they let us in anyway.

Once inside, we went to the room where the bodies were on the cooling boards. Mind you, this was a windowless room. So what else was there to do? My devilish Brother AD turned off the lights.

Instantly, this previously well-lit room became pitch black and was in our young minds transformed into a graveyard. Lord have mercy!

Hysterically, I began screaming, shouting and running blindly in the darkness. I was accidentally hitting and bumping into bodies, desperately trying to get out of the room.

Meanwhile, outside, a man was trying to get away from the police. He ran into the funeral home and lay on a couch in the front room pretending to be dead. When he heard the commotion coming from the room where we were, he himself became frightened. "Mr. Hanley, is that you back there? Is that you?" said the fugitive.

When we heard his voice, we assumed it was coming from one of the bodies. We became even more frantic. Finally, one of the employees of the funeral home came to investigate and turned the lights on, clearing everything up. Scared to death, we returned home for dinner. Of course, we acted as if nothing had happened.

Our idyllic childhood could not last forever. Eventually the reality of the segregated South reared its ugly head. An event occurred that would form the basis of one of ML's most significant philosophical beliefs.

Since our home was a favorite gathering place, ML, AD, and I could often be found in the backyard playing with other neighbor-hood kids, two of whom were little white boys who lived on our street. They were the children of the family that ran the corner gro-cery store. For several years, ML and the boys had been nearly insep-arable playmates. At some point, however, their parents began to come up with excuses for why they could not join in when ML went over to play. ML was perplexed by this turn of events, as any child would be. When he couldn't make sense of it, he went to Mother. In his book *Stride Toward Freedom*, he described what she told him:

> *She took me on her lap and began telling me about slavery and how it had ended with the Civil War. She tried to explain the divided sys-tem of the South—the segregated schools, restaurants, theaters, hous-ing, the White and Colored signs on the drinking fountains, waiting rooms, lavatories—as a social condition rather than a natural order. Then she said the words that almost every Negro hears before he can yet understand the injustice that makes them necessary: You are as good as anyone.*

ML's response to this would ultimately be the foundation of his successful leadership in the civil rights movement.

Growing up on "Sweet" Auburn Avenue was both fun and a life-shaping experience. The phrase "Sweet Auburn" was coined by the late John Wesley Dobbs, father of my classmate and friend June Dobbs Butts and grandfather of Maynard Holbrook Jackson, who in 1974 was elected Atlanta's mayor, the first African American mayor of a major southern American city. "Sweet" Auburn un-abashedly denoted Auburn's status as "the richest Negro street in the world."

The prosperity of this neighborhood owes much to the foresight and vision of a black entrepreneur named Hemon Perry. In 1913, Mr. Perry formed the Standard Life Insurance Company, which quickly became the crown jewel of Auburn's businesses. The Auburn business district grew to include cleaners, banks, funeral homes, nightclubs, and a hotel.

The Atlanta Life Insurance Company was, and still is, critical to Auburn Avenue. In 1905 a former slave, Alonzo Herndon, who also owned several elite barbershops, formed Atlanta Life. It became the second-largest African American insurance company in the world. It recently acquired the securities brokerage business started by Maynard Jackson when he left politics to go into the private sector.

The neighborhood was always abuzz with activity. Jazz was a constantly flowing presence coming from the shops and clubs. Other businesses flourished, including Yates and Milton Drugstore, whose soda fountain had the best sundaes in town, Henry's Grill, Citizens' Trust Bank, the Royal Peacock and Top Hat nightclubs, and the Savoy Hotel. The Savoy was important because it was one of the few hotels that provided lodging for the black entertainers performing in Atlanta. Duke Ellington, Sam Cooke, Jackie Wilson, Ray Charles, and B. B. King, I am sure, all stayed there. Atlanta, of course, was a must-stop date on their tours. There was nothing like it in their hometowns, or in most of the other cities to which they traveled.

In 1976, Sweet Auburn was granted National Historic Landmark status.

As I've said, education was always a key factor in our lives. I started my formal schooling at the Yonge Street Elementary School. One humorous episode accompanied me. I'm about a year and a half older than ML, so when I was six years old and ready to start school, he wasn't old enough to enroll. Because we were so close, and because he always competed with me in everything, he begged Mother to let him go to school when I did. She finally relented, and off we went.

His initial stint in grade school proved short. It lasted from when we started the year in the fall of 1933 until shortly after January 15, 1934. A teacher heard him boasting to some of the other kids about his birthday cake and the "five big candles on it." Once his true age was confirmed, he was sent home until he reached the required age.

The Yonge Street School is historically significant. The first black Parent Teacher Association (PTA) in the United States was organized there, by Selena Sloan Butler, whose son was a student.

Yonge's PTA proved very active. In 1929, Mrs. Butler was appointed by President Herbert Hoover to participate in a White House conference on child health and protection.

Both ML and I eventually went on to new schools when we each reached third grade. I left Yonge and transferred to Oglethorpe Elementary School. He also left Yonge and went to David T. Howard Colored Elementary School.

It was near his sixth-grade graduation ceremony that ML acquired one of his earliest nicknames.

Mother bought him a brown tweed suit for the occasion. It had baggy legs and it tightened at the ankles. We called them "draped suits" or "drapes." At another point, they came to be known as "zoot suits."

He loved that suit. He wore it everywhere he could. He wore it so often that his friends started calling him "Tweed." The name stuck with him for several years.

When I graduated from Oglethorpe after completing sixth grade, I went on to Atlanta University's Laboratory High School. "Lab High" was a concept not unlike today's charter schools. It was an experimental, private institution, run by Atlanta University during the height of segregation. It existed to furnish an advanced liberal education to its students in a supportive, challenging, intensely personal environment.

Lab High closed in 1942, before I started my tenth-grade year, so I went on to Booker T. Washington High School to complete my early schooling. As I detailed earlier, my grandfather Reverend A. D. Williams was instrumental in the school's creation. He led a campaign of public opposition to force the Atlanta city government to provide for the educational needs of black children. Before its opening, there was no public high school in this city for the "Negro" community. ML also attended Booker T. Washington High School. AD went to Palmer Memorial Institute in Sedalia, North Carolina. It was an outstanding private school.

Washington High School sits on twenty-one acres of land. The building was designed by Atlanta architect Eugene C. Wachendorff, and incorporates both medieval and Byzantine elements. The entrance boasts five arches arranged in two tiers using terra cotta and twisted columns. An exact replica of the Booker T. Washington monument from Tuskegee University is placed majestically at the front of the building. The inscription reads, "He lifted the veil of ignorance from his people and pointed the way to progress through education and industry."

While in high school, I was not interested in dating. Even if I had been, it wouldn't have really mattered. My parents, a strict, no-nonsense Baptist minister and his conservative wife, kept a close eye on us. That went double for me, as the only girl. Some of my childhood friends would probably claim that my parents watched me liked hawks. This is not entirely true. Nevertheless, it certainly is not much of an overstatement.

THE KING SIBLINGS AS TEENAGERS: MY BROTHER ML, ME, AND OUR BABY BROTHER, AD. EVEN THEN I HAD A "THING" FOR STYLISH HATS.

Back in those days, dating was an entirely different ballgame. Young women had to be chaperoned, even well into their late teens. It was entirely unheard of for a sixteen-year-old girl to leave home to go on a "date" with a young man. It simply was not acceptable. The most one of us could hope for was to sit on the porch before dusk with her gentleman caller. Boys who lacked manners, or, heaven forbid, whose parents were not known to mine, by both their first and last names—did not make it past the front gate, let alone the front yard.

Like most teenagers, I was especially close to a special group of friends. They included Juanita Sellers, June Dobbs, and Dolores Robinson. Occasionally the subject of boys came up. Dolores and I occasionally talked about them. But in all honesty, it never amounted to more than innocent chitchat. We discussed things like which church they attended; how well they did in school; whether they were good athletically; if they were country bumpkins newly moved to the city; and of course, how well they dressed—that is, whether they were "sharp as tacks" or not.

It's true we talked about boys. However, we did not do much talking on the telephone. Teenagers weren't really allowed to talk on the phone the way they do now. Today, there are cell phones for everyone, including six-year-old kids.

No more, "Number please! . . . Number please!" which is what the operator used to say when a call was placed. The operator actually dialed the number for you.

All I can say is, "It's a different world."

Let me be clear—Dolores Robinson was something else! She was more outgoing than I was. In fact, I vividly recall the time she and her sister Jean stayed with us for a period. During this time, Dolores masterminded and instigated many of our activities outside the house. She was the one who convinced me to ask my parents for permission to do whatever we were able to jointly conceive. Sometimes we succeeded, sometimes not. But it certainly was a lot of fun having the Robinson girls in the house.

We went to school together. We studied together. And, of course, we got into trouble together. Our punishment, when caught, usually consisted of having to get up before school and clean the house. This presented all sorts of challenges. Most teenagers do not want to get up at a regularly scheduled, customary time—and certainly not any earlier.

On one such occasion, I, along with Dolores, Jean, ML, and AD, had gone to a party and failed to return by Daddy's curfew. Kitchen duty was the prescribed punishment. We went to the kitchen to start cleaning up. I doubt the sun had even risen. ML went into a bathroom, as was his style, to avoid helping at all. AD took a place standing by the ironing board.

Jean and I had turned on the radio, down low so that we could barely hear it, so as not to disturb my folks. Jean and I were moving around the kitchen slowly, to say the least. Actually, as I recall, we were probably sitting at the kitchen table. Dolores was cleaning as she had been instructed. Suddenly, we heard Dad coming down the stairs to check on us. Jean and I hopped up from the table and got into high gear. Naturally, AD didn't hear a thing. Dad ultimately found him asleep on the ironing board. He ended up getting a spanking from Daddy on the "seat of his understanding." When ML, now in the bathroom, heard the commotion, he started moving around very noisily—flushing the toilet, turning on every faucet he could find, anything he could do to make noise to prove he was cleaning.

Those were truly fun times with friends and family. I fondly recall our time with our uncle Joel, who also stayed with us for a period. He was Dad's younger brother. Although he was older than us, he was still young. He was just starting college. He went on to become a minister. I remember that Dad would spank Uncle Joel just as he did the boys. We all liked Uncle Joel because he was so close to us in age that he would get into trouble just like us.

Uncle Joel liked my cakes. It was during my teenage years that I began cooking and found that I rather enjoyed it. Once, going down the street from the house, I found a cake recipe just lying on the ground. When I got home, I told my grandmother I wanted to make the cake, which I did. The cake turned out really well. I even put icing on it. Everyone enjoyed it, especially Uncle Joel.

3

SPELMAN AND MOREHOUSE COLLEGE DAYS

pelman College was founded 127 years ago, in April 1881, by Sophia B. Packard and Harriet E. Giles, as the Atlanta Baptist Female Seminary, in the basement of Atlanta's Friendship Baptist Church, which was pastored by Reverend Frank Quarles. A year later, John D. Rockefeller pledged $250 in support of the fledgling institution. In 1884, the name was changed to Spelman Seminary, in honor of Laura Spelman, the wife of John D. Rockefeller, and her parents, Ohio abolitionists Harvey Buel Spelman and Lucy Henry Spelman, whose home served as a stop on the Underground Railroad. Finally, in 1924, the last name change occurred when the seminary became Spelman College.

After I graduated from Washington High School in 1944, there really wasn't much doubt that I'd be continuing the family legacy and tradition by enrolling at Spelman. My mother, grandmother, and a great-aunt all preceded me there. Years later, my daughter, Angela, and my niece Bernice would also become Spelman alumnae. My granddaughter, Farris Christine Watkins, attended Spelman's nursery school. I suspect that as she approaches college age, she'll also be considering Spelman. She's currently twelve years old and tells us that she wants to be an attorney. We have no doubt she will achieve that goal, and we believe a Spelman diploma is likely to grace her office wall.

My connection to Spelman dates to well before my attendance as a student. As I child, I also attended Spelman's nursery school. I fondly remember the wonderful aroma of the rye bread baked daily on the premises. I recall the kind ladies who worked at the nursery reading to us, and the games we played before being put down for our naps.

At sixteen, I eagerly anticipated this new phase of my life. As I prepared for my freshman year, I found that I had been waiting for the opportunity to face the challenges of college and carry on the family's Spelman tradition in the same way a child waits for Christmas day.

At that time, Spelman required its senior students to be housed in the on-campus dormitories. While I did eventually move onto the campus, because I was a city student, I didn't do so until the beginning of my senior year. I loved the experience. Even though my parents' home was no more than fifteen minutes away by car, this was the first time I had lived away from them. It was my first time not sleeping in the bed I'd known since childhood. I got a sense of being removed—almost as if I was in a different city.

College was an exercise in assuming new responsibilities. It provided a new sense of independence. For the first time in my life, I didn't have Mother and Daddy telling me what to do, or when to do it. I had to use the common sense I was born with and the lessons they'd taught me to make my own decisions. It was up to me to work out how much research to put into my class projects; how late

I could stay up and what time to rise each morning; how to schedule my homework and organize my days. In short, I was learning what it meant to be an adult.

One of my first challenges involved mandatory attendance at the five-day-a-week, Monday through Friday 8:00 A.M. chapel in Sisters Chapel. A proctor was placed in the balcony to take attendance. If a student's assigned seat was empty at the appointed hour, a deduction to the student's cumulative grade point average was made. My being present at eight o'clock in the morning required a sometimes mad dash to the streetcar line for the twenty-minute ride to campus from my parent's home. I fulfilled this requirement every school day for all of my four years at Spelman.

Fortunately, for me, by the time I came along, Spelman had done away with one other responsibility it once imposed on all students—rising at 4:30 A.M. to wash and iron clothes.

As I am definitely not an early bird, this would probably never have worked. I'm definitely a night owl. However, another tradition concerning ironing and domestic skills still existed during my time as a student. Every Spelman woman had to demonstrate her ability to iron a skirt and a dresser scarf (the lace material, similar to a doily, that used to be routinely placed on dressers). This exam took place near the end of the senior year and was a requirement for graduation. The exercise was graded by employees of the campus laundry, and in order to pass, the material that one had ironed had to be wrinkle free and could not have "cat faces" appear on it.

Classes were challenging, but I had always been a good student. This didn't change once I reached college. I did well in the classroom and was active socially. I made friends easily, which is not the case for all students. I was fortunate that my two friends from high school, Dolores Robinson and Juanita Sellers, were there on campus with me. I was voted "Most Distinguished Student" by my peers. I was a member of the renowned Glee Club all four years that I was a student; I also performed as a soloist. I participated in the Morehouse-Spelman Chorus. I took part in the English and French clubs and was an active member of the NAACP and YWCA. I honored my family's Spelman legacy as a member of the Granddaughters Club.

During the summers, I worked at the Citizens' Trust Bank. This job afforded me my first exposure to, and the beginning of my foundation in, the worlds of business and finance. It was here that I grasped the lesson that "numbers don't lie." This concept has continued to serve me well, particularly in my roles as vice chair and treasurer of the Martin Luther King, Jr., Center for Nonviolent Social Change and as a member of Ebenezer's Finance Committee.

As a young adult I was blessed to have the caring guidance and support of a number of mentors, all giants in their own right. At the bank, I was taken under the wing of L. D. Milton, president of Citizens' Trust, and fellow employees Thelma Archer, Ruth Naylor, and Juanita Hill. In the larger community, my influences and mentors included Lottie Watkins, businesswoman extraordinaire; businessman J. B. Blayton, the first African American in Georgia to gain a CPA license and my accounting professor; Clayton Yates, co-owner of Yates and Milton Drugstore; C. A. Scott, editor of the *Atlanta Daily World*, one of the nation's oldest African American newspapers; John Wesley Dobbs, activist and a leader in the Prince Hall Masons; attorney A. T. Walden; Warren Cochrane of the Butler Street YMCA; and Dr. Marque Jackson, our family physician and a member of Ebenezer.

I graduated from Spelman College in 1948 with a Bachelor of Arts degree in Economics. For the record, and as I will discuss later, I returned to my alma mater as a professor. I am currently the longest-serving faculty member on campus, having devoted fifty years of my life to Spelman College.

In the same way that my family has a relationship with Spelman spanning the generations, so, too, do we have a long-term relationship with all-male Morehouse College. My grandfather, A. D. Williams, was the first of our line to receive a Morehouse degree. In fact, he was among the first ten men to receive a Morehouse diploma. My father, and of course my brothers, were distinguished alumni. ML's sons, Martin III and Dexter, AD's sons, Reverends Derek and Vernon, and my son, Isaac Jr., are all Morehouse men.

The tenacity and dedication required to obtain a college education are impressive and worthy of praise whenever and however they occur. However, some situations are more impressive and challenging than others.

In Granddad's case, one must remember the tenor of the times. The Ku Klux Klan's reign of terror was at its height. Certainly a black man with the temerity to reject a life of subservience and seek instead intellectual uplift exposed himself and his family to harassment—threats to employment security and personal safety, attacks on the home, and even worse. Lynching was a frequent occurrence. For the masses of black folk, simply acquiring the ability to read and write was extraordinarily difficult. But A. D. Williams, with his roots in rural Greene County, Georgia, was indeed up to the task. His effort was rewarded in 1898, when he was granted his diploma.

The backstory that precedes my father's Morehouse enrollment is at once tender and sad. As I discussed earlier, while Dad was courting Mother, he was a student at Bryant Preparatory School. He was just shy of his twenty-first birthday when it became necessary for Bryant to administer a diagnostic test to determine at what grade level he should be placed.

I can only imagine his emotions, but Dad was flabbergasted when the test results showed him to be at the fifth-grade level. The bottom line was that, at twenty-one, Dad was just going to have to put aside his pride and stubborness, if he expected to complete Bryant and have the opportunity to further his education. I'm proud to say that is exactly what he did. He squeezed himself into desks made for children, certainly not for fully grown men. He got to work, viewed his situation as temporary, and did what he had to do in order to catch up. His dedication, perseverance, and hard work paid off.

He made his way to Morehouse, from the humble beginnings of Stockbridge, Georgia, and flourished. He not only went on to graduate in 1930 with a degree in Theology; he also was elected to and served for many years on the Morehouse College Board of Trustees.

The story of ML's getting to Morehouse once again involves his competitive streak. He had just completed his sophomore year at Washington High. Not to be out-

MY FATHER, REVEREND MARTIN LUTHER KING, SR., WHO WAS UNIVERSALLY KNOWN AS DADDY KING. THIS PHOTOGRAPH IS OF HIM IN HIS MOREHOUSE COLLEGE CAP AND GOWN AT HIS GRADUATION IN 1930.

done by his big sister's graduation, he was among a group, which included my friends June Dobbs and Juanita Sellers, who sat for a new test offered by the administration that would allow successful rising juniors to be admitted directly into college.

You can probably guess the result. This determined, excited fifteen-year-old ML was admitted to Morehouse College in fall 1944 with his mind set on a career in either law or medicine.

The summer before he started Morehouse, ML went off to work in the tobacco fields of Simsbury, Connecticut. The summer of 1944 was important and proved pivotal in his life. It contributed to a deepening and a new clarity in his thinking.

It was his first time out of the segregated South, and consequently, it represented his first opportunity to sample the feeling of relief and a certain freedom that came with being in the "liberated" North. Many years later, as an adult, he reflected on his return to Atlanta at summer's end. He said, "It was a bitter feeling going back to segregation. It was hard to understand why I could ride wherever I pleased on the train from New York to Washington, and then had to change to a Jim Crow car at the nation's capital in order to continue the trip to Atlanta."

When he got back home, there was something markedly different about him. He had undergone a sociological and philosophical metamorphosis. In short, my little brother had become a young man.

But before he became the man the world eventually came to know, there were certain rough edges, which Morehouse was called upon to smooth out. To illustrate this point, I am including, unedited, the text of certain correspondence ML sent my mother that summer. His writings are herewith presented exactly as they were prepared all those years ago. What follows is his response to a letter from Mother informing him that he had successfully passed his exam for Morehouse admission:

Dear Mother

I received your letter and was very glad to hear from you.

I was very glad to hear that I can enter Morehouse. I cannot get home until the 15ths" Because I signed the to leave the 12th and if I leave before the 12th I cannot get my railroad fare and they are also giving us a bonus for about $25.00 if I leave before the 12th I cant get nither of them. I asked Mr. Dansby about entering school late and he said he would see Dean and explain it to him it is a lot of boys here that are entering late. Mr. Dansby is giving some of the boys the Math test here and they won't have to take it when they get there I think I will take it. I will leave here Sept 12 Tues after next and get home the 15th" because I am stoping in N York/or about a day.

ML.

He also wrote her detailing some of his adventures. The letter reads:

Dear Mother Dear:

I received your letter to-day and was very glad to hear from you.

Yesterday we didn't work so we went to Hardford we really had a nice time there. I never though that a person of my race could eat anywhere but we ate in one of the finest rest-u- rant in Hardford And we went to the largest shows there. It is really a large city. Tell AD I hope him luck in summer school. Be sure to tell Christine write me and tell me about the test while you are gone.

AFTER GRADUATION WITH MY
MOTHER AND FATHER.

On our way here we stoped in Spartinburgh S. C. and it is a pretty large place. And we also saw many large ships some as large as the Bethel Church and larger we also saw many airplanes. We went under the Hudson river and entered New York. It is the largest place I have ever seen in my life. We might go there the 4th of July or either Boston Mass they are both near here. The sun has begun to get pretty hot, But that is not the beginning they say it is going to be so hot here in July that you can hardly take it but I am going to take it some day how.

I am very I didn't tell you about the locks but I just forget it. I received And thank you very much. My job in the kitchen is very easy I just do the extra Work I give out the lunches and serve what ever they have to drink. Please send me Mrs. Burney's address and other members.

As head of the religious Dept. I have to take charge of the Sunday Service I have to speak from any text I want to. Be sure to send me my Drivers Ticket.

Mother dear I want you to send me some fried chikens and rolls it will not be so much. And also send my brown shoes the others have worn out.

Mother I cant send but ten dollars home this week because they

*took out for railroad fare and boad it will be the same for the next
two week. We are going to get a raise to five or six dollar in July.*

Your son,

ML.

Once the school year started, it was not until the end of his
freshman year that ML decisively turned toward the ministry. Although this change was quite unexpected and came as a surprise to
the family, he proved to be quite serious about it. Even though he
loved to dance, he began staying in his dorm room and studying
the Bible. This withdrawal from the social scene did not last too
long. Nevertheless, he was sincere, and I imagine it is what he believed he needed to do to prepare for the ministry.

ML AND I GRADUATE ON THE SAME
DAY IN 1948 FROM SPELMAN AND
MOREHOUSE COLLEGE
RESPECTIVELY.

MAY 1948, A PROUD FATHER AND
HIS SON AT ML'S COLLEGE
GRADUATION.

In hindsight, my father credited the wise leadership and counsel of Dr. Benjamin E. Mays, president of Morehouse, and his "enormous gift of speech" and "great communicative powers" as tremendous influences on ML, as major factors in his accepting the call to ministry. Years later, following his assassination, it was Dr. Mays who delivered Martin's eulogy during the portion of his funeral service conducted at Morehouse.

4

GRADUATE SCHOOL

*A*t the time I graduated from Spelman, there was not a doubt in my mind that if I wished to continue my educational pursuits at the master's degree level, I would have to leave the state of Georgia. Even more challenging and frightening, of course, was the prospect that I'd have to leave the comfort and security of my family. The reason for this was frustratingly apparent. The University of Georgia did not admit its first black students until the mid-1960s. In 1948, I simply was not going to be able to enroll in the state's flagship university.

Even at that point, I knew I wanted to pursue my future armed with a graduate degree. I knew this would be a way of acquiring the credentials I would need for future success. But more than that, in the prevailing environment, I knew I'd have to get the kind of credentials, background, and experience that would not permit a discriminatory, racist system in the city of Atlanta or the state of Georgia to deny me the job opportunities to which I would otherwise be entitled.

Hence my decision to attend New York's Columbia University.

A bit of context is in order here to help one to truly understand the times. Not long after the Supreme Court's 1954 landmark decision in *Brown* v. *Board of Education*, Georgia's segregationist governor, Ernest Vandiver, called a special meeting with approximately fifty of the state's chief movers and shakers to discuss the option of shutting down the University of Georgia rather than integrating it, pursuant to the *Brown* directives. It was not until 1961, a full seven years later, that the university admitted its first two black students: Hamilton E. Holmes and Charlayne Hunter. Holmes went on to a distinguished career practicing medicine in Atlanta; Hunter became the award-winning television journalist most closely identified with PBS's nightly *MacNeil/Lehrer Report*.

There is more to this story of the University of Georgia's being barred to prospective black students. They actually went the extra mile to insure that was the case. From today's vantage point, when a woman and an African American can credibly compete for the highest office in the land, it's hard to comprehend how warped and sick the racial environment was. The state of Georgia actually maintained and funded a taxpayer-supported program pursuant to which it would pay the full costs—tuition, room, board, transportation—of black students who wished to attend graduate school . . . provided it was out of state, thus insuring the preservation of the all-white halls of the University of Georgia. In what truly must rank as an example of the benefits of unintended consequences, I was afforded the opportunity to pursue a graduate degree at Columbia University, a far more prestigious institution, rather than simply attending my own home state school on an integrated basis.

Once ML completed Morehouse, Daddy fully supported his decision to continue his education. That fall, at age nineteen, he announced that he was off to Crozer Theological Seminary in Chester, Pennsylvania, a small town just outside Philadelphia. I'm sure Daddy didn't think he necessarily needed to go that far from home, but they both knew the future beckoned. Soon thereafter, ML became one of eleven black students in the entire seminary, over half of whom were in his entering freshman class. The entire student body consisted of fewer than one hundred students. So that fall he joined me in heading off for a northern graduate school.

It was tragic, sad, and unfortunately the way things were.

As the day approached for me to depart Atlanta, bound for Columbia, there was much discussion in our house about New York. Daddy could not stress enough how cold it would be. He constantly reminded Mother to make sure I had enough warm clothes packed, so I wouldn't go up there and "freeze to death."

He also spent a good bit of time talking to me about boys. He lectured me about the young fellows that lived in the North, telling me how "slick" they were and that I should be "on my toes" at all times. He said he would make sure that ML would check on me in New York as often as he could from Crozer.

At one point, I was upstairs putting the finishing touches on my packing. It was the night before I was to leave, and I wanted to make sure I wasn't forgetting anything. I heard my mother calling out for me.

I ran out of my room and stood at the top of the stairs. Mother Dear had a serious look on her face.

"Ma'am?" I said.

"Come downstairs for a minute. I want to talk to you. I won't keep you long. Then you can go back up and finish your packing."

I headed downstairs with absolutely no idea what she wanted.

When we sat on the couch, she took my hands in her own and placed them gently on her lap.

"Christine, you know, New York is a lot different from Atlanta. Northerners are different from us southerners. They do things differently. Your father and I want you to be on your best behavior and we know that you will. Remember, well-brought-up young ladies are always supposed to act accordingly."

"Yes, ma'am."

Mother went on for another five or ten minutes, telling me what to wear and when to wear it. She talked about how to behave, as if I didn't already know. I suppose, like all mothers, she just wanted to make sure that when I met strangers, I'd be at my best. She reminded me yet again to be polite and to always say "thank you."

I listened intently, but remained mostly silent during our chat. When Mother Dear finished, we embraced and I returned upstairs to finish packing.

That night I tossed and turned. Thoughts about my trip and living away from home and away from Atlanta for the first time kept interrupting my sleep.

The next morning, Juanita Sellers and I boarded the Silver Comet train, bound for the biggest city in the United States—New York. I was a bundle of anxious nerves. I was excited, yet somewhat sad to be leaving my family.

Our parents had packed us food, but we ate our meals in the train's dining car. The dining cars, naturally, were segregated. We were separated from the white passengers by two curtains, so, for the duration of the trip, we took our meals in the "Colored Dining Car."

Being in New York would be a first for both Juanita and me. We were both thrilled and excited. We knew it'd be different from Atlanta, but we probably weren't prepared for how great the differences would be. For example, there was the whole prospect of the subway. Until that point, my experience with public transportation had been limited to the streetcar line. Then, too, there was my defining New York experience with the original "fast food"—dining at the Automat. I was used to eating at my parents' dining room table, and, occasionally, in a restaurant. This whole prospect of pre-cooked, already prepared dishes, lined up in machines for inspection like new cars on an auto dealer's lot, was something new, fun, and exciting. Each day, by simply inserting a few coins in a slot, I'd have breakfast, lunch, or dinner, hot, steaming, and at my fingertips. I loved it.

When we arrived, we didn't actually start out living on the Columbia University campus. Instead, we were housed at the Emma Ransom House YWCA on Harlem's 137th Street. We remained there for two years before finally moving into on-campus dormitory rooms.

Having been given instructions from our parents not to go beyond the areas of New York that were absolutely necessary, we hadn't really had a chance to take in all there was to see. We could, however, as a consolation explore all these places when my brother came from Crozer to visit. I promptly wrote Martin a terse letter asking him to come visit soon. I left out the superfluous details, such as Daddy's forbidding any explorations of the city until he came to town.

I do recall one visit, in particular. When Martin arrived from Crozer, he was not alone. He brought along one of his closest friends, Walter McCall, whom he had known during their days together at Morehouse. As a college student, Walter had been a barber on campus to earn much-needed money for school. He was now at Crozer Seminary with ML studying theology.

They took the train up from Philadelphia and made their way to Ransom House. Juanita and I waited like giddy schoolgirls for their arrival. We took in all New York had to offer. We visited museums and Times Square, and marveled at the kind of skyscrapers you had to crane your neck to see. Later that year, my parents also visited me when Daddy came to New York for a meeting of the Morehouse Board of Trustees.

Suffice it to say, when I actually did set foot on the Columbia campus I was blown away. It was quite an experience. The school has a rich history of academic excellence, and unlike the South, it promoted diversity from the start. Columbia was like a small city unto itself. Everything a student could need was right there. The lawns were green and neatly manicured. There were trees all across the campus, which was a nice touch. It reminded me of home. The students, who literally came from across the world, were bright and eager to learn. The libraries were fantastic. I was in academic heaven. I could see myself getting lost in the stacks for weeks at a time.

My first semester at Columbia was the worst of my life. I started out as an economics major. I was the only black and the only female in the class. My professor—naturally, a white male—was not the least bit interested in acknowledging my raised hand, or in my questions. Eventually I was joined by a black male whose last name was Gayles—whose first name I can't recall. Nothing changed. The professor had no appreciation of either of us as students. Neither of us did very well in the class. At the semester's end, we both transferred from the class. I immediately changed my major to the social foundations of education.

During that initial semester, ML wrote several letters to our mother informing her of my difficulty in the class and how upsetting it had become for me.

After Daddy learned of my experience, he said, "Christine, you can always come home." Returning home and not completing my graduate degree was never a consideration. Though the experience was very much a challenge and upsetting, I was determined not to allow it to dictate the remainder of my graduate experience.

The next semester and the remainder of my tenure were totally different. Things were much better. I settled into the routine, did well in my new field, and found myself making new friends and adapting to life in the Big Apple. I even found myself rushing through the streets along with the native New Yorkers. I also made trips to Philadelphia to visit ML, who always was supportive and encouraging.

In 1949, Columbia University awarded me my first Master's Degree in Social Foundations of Education. Over the next few summers I went back and earned a second master's degree in special education.

It was at Crozer that ML became serious about his studies, much more so than he had been at Morehouse. His intellectual curiosity was sharpened, focused, and challenged. He enjoyed the beautiful campus and erudite atmosphere immensely. He also enjoyed frequent dinners at the home of Reverend Dr. J. Pius Barber, who was a Morehouse man, and Crozer's first black graduate. These dinners provided additional mental stimulation and allowed for intellectual debate and spirited conversation.

Crozer is where ML also began collecting all the works of Mohandas K. Gandhi that he could find. He'd heard a Gandhi lecture in Philadelphia, delivered by Dr. Mordecai Johnson, president of Howard University. In addition to Gandhi's works, he also read Henry David Thoreau's *Civil Disobedience* while attending Crozer. These intellectual giants would serve to inspire him as he conducted his nonviolent campaigns across the South for the remainder of his career. ML excelled in all aspects of student and campus life. He was elected president of his senior class, becoming the first black Crozer student to serve in this capacity.

In June 1951, Martin graduated valedictorian of his class. At graduation, he was awarded the Pearl Ruth Plafker Fellowship for graduate study, which was presented annually to the "Most Outstanding member of the Graduating Class." He applied to doctoral programs at both Yale and Boston universities. He was accepted by both. He chose Boston, in order to study directly under the personalist theologians on the faculty whom he had come to admire while at Crozer, among them Dr. Edgar S. Brightman and Dr. L. Harold DeWolf.

Dr. Brightman had published two books Martin was exposed to at Crozer, *The Finding of God* and *A Philosophy of Religion*. He drew on them for various essays he was required to write.

In fall 1951, Martin entered Boston University's School of Theology to pursue his Ph.D. studies. Dr. Brightman became Martin's primary mentor. When he died in 1953, Dr. DeWolf assumed the role of his principal mentor. The perspective advocated and advanced by personalism appealed to ML because of its critical emphasis on the individual.

While at Boston, he took a course at Harvard and studied the modern existentialist philosophers: Martin Heidegger, Karl Jaspers, and Jean-Paul Sartre. He would also study the Danish philosopher Søren Kierkegaard, who also focused heavily on the individual.

In spring 1955, Boston University awarded Martin his Ph.D. in Systematic Theology.

Later he would write, "This personal idealism remains today my basic philosophical position. Personalism's insistence that only personality—finite and infinite—is ultimately real, strengthened me in two convictions; it gave me metaphysical and philosophical grounding for the idea of a personal God, and it gave me a metaphysical basis for my belief in the dignity and worth of all human personality."

In hindsight, it's clear that this twin focus—"the idea of a personal God" coupled with the belief in "the dignity and worth of all human personality"—would form the basis of Martin's ministry as he was launched into the forefront of the civil rights movement, and in all his struggles and battles that were yet on the horizon.

5

MY FIRST REAL JOB AT W. H. CROGMAN

*M*y first professional job was as a teacher at W. H. Crogman Elementary School in Atlanta. As was the case with much of my life, this accomplishment did not come without challenge and struggle. I had trouble getting hired by the Atlanta public school system. It took me two applications and the intervention of my father with the mayor before I was offered a job.

It turned out that my application was rejected as an act of retaliation because of my father's involvement, years earlier, in the struggle to bring about equality of pay for black teachers and their white counterparts. Daddy and his supporters ultimately prevailed, and black teachers eventually received the same pay as whites, but the entrenched forces of racism and discrimination did not take defeat lightly. Nor did they forget—they did not intend to make life easy for the daughter of the man who had triumphed on the pay issue.

I had already received my first Columbia degree when I first applied for employment with the Atlanta public schools. This first application was denied. I then reapplied. Once again, I was denied. It was only at this point that suspicions began to enter my mind. I knew that I was well qualified, but as you would expect, I began to harbor doubts about ever obtaining a position in Atlanta.

Then, one day, I went to visit Mrs. Bazoline Usher, who was employed by the Atlanta School Board in the capacity of Chief Supervisor of Negro Teachers. She was a courageous woman and clearly, by making the decision to speak with me, she was endangering her job.

She informed me that my applications had been routinely filed away in a cabinet and that the white powers that be had no intention of hiring me because of my father's activism. To put it mildly, Daddy hit the roof when I informed him of what I had learned from Ms. Usher.

As always, he thought carefully and planned his approach. His next actions were measured and political.

He picked up the phone and called Mayor William B. Hartsfield. After having a conversation about their joint political struggles, past and present, Daddy informed the mayor about my job search and the difficulties I had experienced. When he finished with the story, the mayor told Daddy that he would call him back within the half hour. He also asked my father to have me on the phone when he called back. Within a matter of minutes, the mayor did indeed call back. He informed us that the Atlanta superintendent of schools, Ms. Ira Jarrell, would personally welcome me to a meeting in her office the following day. It was at this meeting that Ms. Jarrell informed me of the offer of a teaching position, at W. H. Crogman Elementary School.

A new school year was to begin in a few short days. Of course, I was ecstatic—overjoyed is more accurate, but the sweetness of the moment was tempered by a bitter realization that not all black folk had a father who could personally speak to the mayor and obtain such swift results. This was an advantage I knew I had, and for which I was grateful.

I knew in my heart that my credentials were more than in order. On merit alone, I know I should have gotten the job without any external influence. But the fact is that's not the way it happened. I didn't get the job without my dad's help, because race was indeed a factor. The year was 1950. At that point, Daddy and others had already spent years working with white leaders to bring about a change in race relations between blacks and whites in Atlanta. The pay-parity struggle was just one battle in that war. The fight was continuing then, and it continues to this day.

Crogman was led by its principal, Mrs. Marian Mitchell. Unlike the majority of other Atlanta schools, Crogman was organized by departments. There was a Department of Math, a Department of Science, and so forth. For me, this innovative, forward-looking approach highlighted Mrs. Mitchell's advanced, creative leadership skills.

I was assigned a seventh-grade reading class with twenty to twenty-five students. One student who stands out in my mind was a young man named Alton Hornsby. He was extraordinarily studious and very serious about his work. Today, that young man is Dr. Alton Hornsby, Fuller E. Calloway Professor of History at Morehouse College. Another student who made quite an impression on me was Jacob Wortham, who went on to become editor of a major New York magazine. Unfortunately, Jacob is now deceased.

All in all, my experience at Crogman was challenging, enjoyable, demanding, and rewarding. It confirmed for me that I had found what I wanted to do with my life: be involved with education and teaching.

6

MY COLLEGE TEACHING CAREER

I began my teaching career at Spelman College in fall 1958. I love this place and all that it stands for. I love and cherish it for all that it means to me and to countless thousands of other alumnae. What a measurable difference this venerable institution has made in my own life, as well as in the lives of young women from literally all across the globe. Spelman is indeed a remarkable institution.

I was hired as the director of the freshman reading program. The program was funded by a grant from the Eli Lily Foundation. Lily simultaneously funded similar programs at the other member schools of the Atlanta University Center: Clark College, Morehouse, Morris Brown College, and Atlanta University. Since that time, Clark College and Atlanta University have merged to create Clark Atlanta University. Each school had an individual program administrator whose duties mirrored mine. Dr. Lynette Saine-Gaines, a professor at Atlanta University, was in charge of its program, and was assisted by Ms. Miriam Jellins. At Morehouse, Dr. Addie Mitchell and Mrs. Emma Brown were program codirectors; Dr. Isabella Butts ran Clark College's program; while Ms. Lavern Graves directed Morris Brown's. The Lily grant also provided for a graduate assistant for each program at the respective schools. This allowed the graduate assistants to support the program directors while they worked for their Master's degrees, majoring in English with an emphasis in reading.

Eventually, the Lily funding for the reading program ended. As it was phased out, Spelman organized the Learning Resources Center as part of the Department of Education. I was appointed director and hold that position today.

The Learning Resources Center is a facility that allows students to perfect skills they need to master, such as comprehensive reading, analytical writing, and various computer applications. We offer innovative workshops and provide interdisciplinary tutors to assist students in enhancing their overall performance and achieving academic goals.

Over these many years at Spelman, it's been my students that have brought me the greatest joy. Many of my former students have gone on to pursue careers in education and have come back and expressed their appreciation to me for all the hard work and effort I demanded of them. And not only that, in my travels across the country and around the world, former students find me and express this same sense of appreciation. They tell me they were well prepared for their chosen fields of endeavor. As you would expect, this has been extremely gratifying and rewarding.

I also had the opportunity to teach young men from Morehouse. I served as an adjunct professor for approximately one year, while filling in for Dr. Addie Mitchell in the reading program as she took a sabbatical to pursue her doctorate at the University of Chicago.

I continue to teach Morehouse students as they cross-register for education classes at Spelman. My students have been both inspiring and challenging. It is purely because of them that I love what I do. It is because of them that I look forward to coming to work every day.

As noted, I am currently the longest-serving faculty member. With the recent retirement of Dr. Joyce Finch Johnson, college organist and former chair of the Music Department, I was left as the lone faculty member with over four decades of service.

The administrations I have served with have all been wonderful. I have been privileged to work with five outstanding presidents: Dr. Albert Manley, Dr. Donald Stewart, Dr. Johnetta B. Cole, Dr. Audrey Manley, and Dr. Beverly D. Tatum, our current president.

There's no question that, at whatever point I choose to retire, it's the students I will miss the most. They've brought so much to the classroom. They've helped to provide me a different outlook on life. I can recall days when, like anyone, I may have been troubled or not feeling one hundred percent. But the moment I set foot in the classroom, all was well with my soul. I forgot my problems and was renewed.

I've often been asked what advice I give my students about launching their careers and going out into the world. It's simple—I tell them, "Always do your absolute best. Your work is a reflection of you and no one else."

7

TAKING SPOUSES AND STARTING FAMILIES

*I*t's no secret that one of best things parents can do for their children is to set good examples in their daily lives. I've always felt that this can best be achieved when the parents actually illustrate the lessons they want their children to grasp through the way they go about leading their lives, in things both great and small. I have no doubt that the fact that all of us, ML, AD, and I, were successful in finding our life partners and in forging strong, secure families is due in no small part to the example Daddy and Mother Dear set during the course of their forty-eight-year marriage.

Although I was the eldest of the siblings, we actually married in reverse chronological order. First came AD and Naomi Barber in 1950. Then, as the world now knows, ML and Coretta Scott in 1952. And, humorously enough, I met my husband, Isaac Newton Farris, in October 1956, while I was on a date with another young man.

Naturally, there's a story here. I was at the wedding reception of another Ebenezer member who had just gotten married. When we arrived, a young music lover named Isaac Farris was there playing records, deejaying, in today's parlance. As the old saying goes, "Timing is everything." The first thing my date did was go to the kitchen in search of something to eat.

Big mistake!

Capitalizing on this opportunity, this handsome, conservatively dressed Mr. Farris came over and introduced himself. Right off the bat he struck me as a pleasant person. We engaged in typical small talk and exchanged the traditional pleasantries. It turned out he was from a small town that I'd never heard of, Eolia, Missouri. It was obvious immediately that his manners were impeccable. It was clear that he was well spoken, and that he must have had a very good upbringing—that he'd been "raised right," as we used to put it. His personality was easy and likeable. Immediately, it seemed as if we'd known each other for years. His smile was warm and soothing. It was the kind of smile that left a lasting impact. It made me imagine a world of future possibilities. He just made me feel good. I must admit that in the back of my mind I was conscious of the fact that, if things ever got that far, he was the type of man I could bring home to meet my folks.

Isaac didn't have a car at the time and I was only too happy to offer him a ride to his place. For the sake of the story's ultimate outcome, I'm thankful that my date was kind enough to oblige. We gave Isaac the ride. I don't believe we exchanged information that night, but of course, I now knew where he lived.

When I got home that evening, I had the feeling something special had just happened. Obviously, there's no way I could have known that Isaac would become my husband, but I knew, without question, he'd left a most favorable impression. There was something sincere and honest about him. He radiated the feeling that he could be trusted. That's no small matter with me, for I am keenly aware that trust is valuable and important and should never be given lightly.

At some point, there comes the time that a daughter takes a serious marital candidate to meet her parents. That time came for me. I don't know whether Isaac was nervous about meeting my parents. I do know he didn't show it to me. He had to go through that time-perfected ritual. He had to meet Dad and win his approval before he ever got the opportunity to meet Mother. It's funny now, but I clearly remember Daddy saying that he had been fully prepared to unleash all his "Papa Bear" rage on Isaac once, after he brought me home a tad late from a date.

We were sitting outside the house in the car past Daddy's deadline. He came out and told Isaac he "should come inside." Isaac was different from some of the other men I'd been out with. Rather than avoiding Daddy or making some feeble excuse, he looked him straight in the eye, said, "Yes, sir," and accepted the invitation to come in and talk.

To make a long story short, Isaac fully redeemed himself. Daddy came to love and accept him as another son. There was nothing Isaac would not do to care for and assist Dad, and we've always loved and respected him for it.

We were married August 19, 1960, at Ebenezer, where my brothers AD And ML conducted the ceremony. All blushing brides think their wedding is a big deal. But just between us, let me assure you—my wedding was a big deal. I had not one, not two, not three, but *five* bridal showers. It's probably more accurate to say that I had a bridal week.

The first shower was hosted by the late Mrs. Esther Smith in her

ISAAC AND I ARE SHOWN ON OUR WEDDING DAY, AUGUST 19,
1960, SLICING THE WEDDING CAKE.

lovely home. The second was held at that world-famous Atlanta
landmark, Paschal's Restaurant. Paschal's is justifiably well known
for its marvelous chicken dinners. It was also the scene of numerous late-night planning meetings and strategy sessions as ML and
the Southern Christian Leadership Conference prepared for their
battles for justice all across the nation. Paschal's started out in a
small trailer on Hunter Street (now Martin Luther King, Jr., Drive),
in a structure with no kitchen. Paschal's is now a million-dollar
business with a location in Atlanta's showcase Hartsfield/Jackson
International Airport. It has a second, recently opened location in
the newly emerging avant-garde Castlebury Hill neighborhood.

My third shower was given by the Ebenezer Church Choir, of which I was a proud member.

My friend Nina Miller gave the fourth shower, which was held at her home in the Wigwam Apartments, near Auburn Avenue and Randolph Street, in the Old Fourth Ward, an area now on the rebound and undergoing rapid gentrification. The fifth and last shower was hosted by Mrs. Gwendolin Keith Hopgood in her home.

As you would expect, I was thrilled and excited about each shower. They were all wonderful, and I have cherished memories of each, all these many, many years later. They were lovingly planned and executed, and I remain indebted to my friends, church organizations, family acquaintances, and everyone who so thoughtfully and graciously made my wedding so memorable.

The wedding rehearsal and its sit-down dinner were held at Ebenezer and were sponsored by our old family friend Mrs. Nanniene Crawford, who had been responsible for helping ML and me get to attend a high school dance despite our dad's protests many, many years earlier.

After all the preliminary activities, the day of the wedding finally arrived. Oddly, what I remember is being at home before the ceremony and peeking out the window and catching a glimpse of Isaac. Everybody knows the old tradition that the bridge and groom aren't supposed to see each other before the ceremony. Nonetheless, it warmed my heart to see him—and I'm glad I did.

There's another old tradition, which involves the groom's giving his bride a gift of pearls. When I looked out that window and saw Isaac, he had the strand of pearls with him.

There was massive construction being done on Interstate 20,

which cuts a swath across the neighborhood where the church is located. For months Auburn Avenue and the streets surrounding Ebenezer had been closed. Coincidentally and, it seemed, just for me, the streets were reopened on the day of the wedding. That certainly made for a relieved bridal party.

As I said, my brothers conducted the ceremony. It was truly a family affair. Isaac's brother George Farris served as his best man. One of his groomsmen was ML's comrade in arms during the civil rights movement, Reverend Ralph David Abernathy, and Mr. Lewis Reed was the other. (It was Mr. Reed's wedding reception I was attending when I met Issac—so I suppose you could say we had come full circle.) My sister-in-law Coretta, ML's wife, was my matron of honor. The maid of honor was my friend Dr. Dolores Robinson. My bridesmaids were my lifelong friend Juanita Sellers (now Juanita Sellers Stone), Eleanor Smith Traylor, whose mother gave one of the bridal showers, Elise Fortsen Gilham, and Lena Johnson McLin.

My sister-in-law Naomi King, AD's wife, was unable to participate. She was in the late stage of pregnancy. The flower girls were ML and AD's daughters, Yolanda and Alveda King, respectively. AD's son, my nephew Alfred King was the ring bearer. The remainder of the wedding party included organist David Stills and candle lighters Laura English Robinson and Patricia Marshall Marks.

THE BRIDE DESCENDING THE STAIRS ON HER WEDDING DAY.

The reception was held in the backyard of my parents' home, in Northwest Atlanta (they had sinced moved from Auburn Avenue), which was decorated beautifully. I recall my parents' garage being so stuffed with gifts that they had to park their cars outside until we could remove all the presents.

The whole day felt like a magical, mystical dream. It seemed as if I had somehow emerged from one of the fairy tales we all grew up knowing. And now, I was destined to live happily ever after. It was wonderful. We honeymooned in Nassau, after an overnight stay in Miami before boarding the cruise ship to the Bahamas.

When I met Isaac, he was a linotypist at the *Atlanta Daily World* newspaper. He later worked in retail management at W. T. Grant and Rich's department stores. Isaac is now a successful entrepreneur here in Atlanta. He has a business called Farris Colorvision

ISAAC AND ME WITH THE WEDDING PARTY.

and has published a photographic history of Atlanta entitled *Scenes of Black Atlanta*.

Two years after the wedding, we started our family. We've been blessed with two wonderful children: Isaac Newton Farris, Jr., who was born April 13, 1962, and his sister, Angela Christine Farris (Watkins), who came along on May 29, 1964. They were both born during the last vestiges of the separate-but-equal era. Hence, they were both delivered at McClendon's Hospital, a private facility owned and operated by Dr. Earl McClendon, an African American physician who maintained a private practice in Atlanta.

Isaac attended Morehouse, not unexpectedly, and now serves as president and chief executive officer of the Martin Luther King, Jr., Center for Nonviolent Social Change. Angela, as I mentioned earlier, is a graduate of Spelman College and is now, like me, a member of the faculty at our alma mater.

Growing up, Isaac Jr. was a typical boy; always getting into one thing or another. From the very beginning, he was a "people person," as the saying goes. There's never been anything shy about him. No way, no how. He would go to anyone as soon as he could walk, and once he learned to talk, he'd strike up a conversation with anybody, whether he knew them or not.

Because he was an adventure seeker, shall we say, belts and spankings figured prominently in his youth. Again, nonviolence had its limits.

Isaac Jr. has always been the outgoing type, and he was bitten by the political bug early on. Like his mother and his uncles ML and AD before him, he went to Oglethorpe Elementary School. He was actually quite the little speaker and politician. He was elected president of the student body.

TO MY LEFT, MY CHILDREN—ISAAC., JR., PRESIDENT AND CEO OF THE MARTIN LUTHER KING, JR., CENTER FOR NONVIOLENT SOCIAL CHANGE, AND DR. ANGELA FARRIS, ASSOCIATE PROFESSOR OF PSYCHOLOGY AT SPELMAN COLLEGE—BOTH IN ATLANTA, GEORGIA.

Because he was fascinated with President Kennedy, he co-opted a famous quotation from Kennedy's Inaugural Address: "Ask not what your country can do for you, ask what you can do for your country."

During his own speech, Isaac told the students, "Ask not what Oglethorpe can do for you, but what you can do for Oglethorpe." The students loved the quotation and erupted in thunderous applause.

On another occasion, after hearing him speak, a staff member, Mrs. Laura Brown, invited him to speak at John F. Kennedy Middle School. This was while he was still in elementary school himself. Even then, Isaac would put together his own speeches without any help from his father or me.

At Douglas High School, he played on the "B" team football squad. Isaac Jr. was also something of an entrepreneur. Along with his cousin Dexter, ML's youngest son, they started a deejay service and together they traveled around the city spinning records at various social events. Isaac and Dexter also liked photography. For a while they made some money from their picture-taking activities. I recall that they photographed a few weddings that took place at Ebenezer.

My daughter, Angela, is a different story and was a different kind of child. She didn't get into the same type or the same amount of trouble as her brother. She was outgoing in a different way. I enrolled her in ballet class, which she loved. She adored the ballerina outfits, and generally loved anything associated with dance.

She's always had an independent streak, and there's one episode I remember in particular. We had gone to an Atlanta Braves game during Hank Aaron's assault on the all-time home run record previously held by Babe Ruth. We were making our way through the crowd. I was holding her hand, as usual. She objected, and wanted to make her way alone. It was simply a case of a child asserting her independence before she was really prepared to do so. Despite my misgivings, I relented, releasing her hand. I allowed her to walk ahead of us, while I kept a careful watch on her—or so I thought.

Before long she had gotten lost in the throng of people in the concourse. I was frantic. Eventually, my husband, together with Mother and Daddy, managed to calm me down long enough to suggest that we just keep walking with the flow of the crowd. After what seemed like years, but was in reality only a few moments, we found her walking alone in the crowd—without a care in the world.

Don't ever let anyone suggest that parenting doesn't have its heart-stopping moments.

Angela was a sensitive child. There were several occasions while she was growing up that were challenging. The incident that follows is the one I found most touching. Like her brother, Angela also attended Oglethorpe Elementary School. Like him, she, too, was involved in student government. She had been vice president and around seventh grade she decided to run for president. I tried to discourage this effort, but she insisted. She campaigned extremely hard against a classmate, Rita Smith, who also was one of her friends. Angela made signs and posters, shook hands, and made speeches. She put her heart into the campaign and was confident that she would win.

But that's not what happened. When the results were announced Angela found that she had lost.

She was devastated and was in a kind of shock. After school that day she went to my father's house, where her dad was to pick her up later. She got into some kind of disagreement with her cousin Alveda, who snapped at her. The pain from her election loss, exacerbated by her argument with Alveda, pretty much sent her over the edge. She told us later that a part of her "just wanted to disappear."

She did what she could as a child. And that was to hide under a table somewhere in the back of the house. When her father arrived to pick her up she was nowhere to be found. Everyone searched the house but they couldn't locate her. When they called me to tell me what was going on, I went into a panic, as any mother would. My husband began to question Isaac Jr., asking if he had done anything to his sister. At that point Angela ran out from her hiding place, because she didn't want her brother to get into trouble.

Later that night at home, we sat her down for a talk. We tried to explain to her that this was why we had tried to discourage her from running for the office. We told her that she would have to keep going and not allow this defeat to prevent her from trying again another day.

The next day Angela's teacher asked her to read something in front of the class.

Determined not to let her classmates see the impact the election had on her, she got up in front of the class and read as if nothing had occurred the day before. However, she was holding all these emotions in and suppressing her very real hurt. As she read, she noticed a new and unfamiliar tremor in her voice. This strange sound in her voice simply would not go away, and it kept recurring. Finally, we took her to an ear, nose, and throat specialist.

The doctor was unable to find anything. From seventh grade until some point after she completed high school, Angela courageously confronted this trembling-voice problem. Then, just as quickly as it began, it ended. In that other children can be unforgiving in their ridicule, this episode was extremely challenging for her. In high school, she often had me write notes to her teachers requesting that they excuse her from oral presentations. Some teachers complied with this request; others did not.

In college, she was able to cope much better. But her self-esteem had been tremendously affected.

Angela has worked diligently at coping with this problem and confronted the world with confidence. I'm so proud of her for her tenacity and dedication. As I said, she successfully completed Spelman, earned her Master's degree, and holds a Ph.D. in educational psychology, both from Georgia State University. One of her professors there—the late, world-renowned Egyptologist Dr. Asa

Hilliard, her mentor and advisor—said that he predicted a successful career for her because of her mastery of social skills. She also holds a seat as an Associate Professor of psychology on Spelman's faculty.

Not only that, she's a mother. This, of course, makes me a grandmother bursting with pride over my granddaughter, Farris Christine Watkins, who joined the family on January 22, 1997. I was privileged to witness her birth, and I can only make the same remark everyone else does who has had such an opportunity. It was simply "a miracle." Nothing in the world compares to witnessing a birth. It was without a doubt one of the most precious moments of my life. There was a bond established in that delivery room between mother, daughter, and granddaughter that spans the generations, and I'm confident will last a lifetime.

Fortunately, both of my brothers were as lucky as me in terms of finding the spouse of their dreams. Each had a long-lasting marriage, which terminated only upon their death. AD, as I noted previously, was the first of us to marry. He met Naomi Barber while he was at Morehouse and she was a high school student at Booker T. Washington. She hailed from Alabama. She was attractive and intelligent and possessed a personality that meshed perfectly with his.

When I look back over some of the episodes in our lives, I'm tempted to say that sometimes it seemed as if there was never a dull moment. For example, ML and I almost missed Naomi and AD's wedding completely. Before the wedding we had traveled to New York from Philadelphia with Deacon Jethro English, who had a sister he wanted to visit in New York City.

It was on the trip back to Atlanta that we ran into trouble. We were traveling by car with ML at the wheel. Before we were able to make it out of Pennsylvania, we were pulled over for speeding. Truth be told, on occasion, ML was known for driving with a lead foot. We were given a ticket and had to follow the officer to either the jail or the courthouse, I don't remember which. ML rode in the back of the police car, Deacon English drove the car ML had been driving, and I was left as his worried front-seat passenger.

When we heard the amount of the fine, we could have fainted! It was a whopping twenty-five dollars. ML had a look on his face that was *priceless* as he glanced from me to Deacon English, and back again. Deacon English didn't have much. And poor ML didn't have a penny to his name. Nobody really had much, but "old reliable" Christine had exactly twenty-five dollars. This assured us our freedom and gave us the opportunity to hightail it to the wedding.

THIS IS AD AND NAOMI'S WEDDING DAY. JOINING THE HAPPY COUPLE ARE A BEAMING BEST MAN, ML, AND ME, ON THE LEFT IN YET ANOTHER HAT CHOSEN FOR THE SPECIAL OCCASION.

By the time we arrived at the ceremony, at Naomi's parents' home on McDaniel Street in Atlanta, the guests were already gathered and seated. That's just how close we cut it.

Again, there was a happy ending, and a wonderful marriage began that day.

To this union, five children were born. They are Alfred D. W. King III, Alveda King, Esther Darlene King, Reverend Vernon Christopher King of Charlotte, North Carolina, and Reverend Derek B. King, of Indianapolis, Indiana. Unfortunately, two of these children have died. We lost Darlene in summer 1976; ten years later, we lost her brother Al, under tragically similar circumstances. They both collapsed and died while jogging.

The whole world knows of Coretta Scott King, and her role as spouse, confidante, freedom fighter, keeper of ML's legacy, founding president of the Martin Luther King, Jr., Center for Nonviolent Social Change, Human Rights activist, and leader in her own right.

What the world doesn't know is their love story. In late January 1952, ML was a student in Boston and Coretta Scott, from Heiberger (now Marion), Alabama, was a student at the New England Conservatory of Music. They had a mutual friend in Spelman alumna Mary Powell, who was married to a nephew of Dr. Benjamin E. Mays, Morehouse's president. She was doing graduate work at the same school as Coretta. Mary had mentioned ML to Coretta, and vice versa. After some convincing, Mary eventually gave ML Coretta's telephone number.

When I think of this, I have to laugh. ML always had a way with words, and apparently the words he used with Coretta during that first conversation made an impact. According to ML, they talked for hours, and clearly there was a mutual attraction. Before he hung up he had asked Coretta for a date.

The next day, anxious to meet her in person, ML drove from Boston University in his green Chevy to pick up Coretta—who had an hour between classes. They had a leisurely lunch date. It was a typical winter day in Massachusetts, cold and crisp. Remember, this was the first time they'd met in person, twenty-four hours after their first telephone conversation.

During lunch, they engaged in a lively, spirited conversation, and ML asked a series of questions. After lunch, as they were return-ing to the conservatory, ML told Coretta, "You have everything I have ever wanted in a wife." From that first meeting, Martin Luther King, Jr., knew he had found a wife in Coretta Scott.

As usual, there were quirks on the way to the fairy tale ending.

Before my parents ever had an opportunity to meet Coretta, Dad had already learned of ML's having "been in the company of an extremely attractive young lady" when he preached at Roxbury's Twelfth Street Baptist Church in Boston. This news reached Daddy courtesy of his good friend Reverend William H. Hester, the church's senior pastor. The purpose of the call had been to inform Daddy what a good job ML had done preaching that Sunday. The com-ment about Coretta was ancillary, but you can bet it was what Dad remembered.

When my folks *did* meet Coretta, it wasn't so much a planned meeting as it was a schemed meeting. It was a total surprise, con-cocted, planned, and orchestrated by Dad. My mother initially ob-jected, but she eventually went along with the plan. It turns out they'd been in New York City for a meeting of the Morehouse Board of Trustees when Daddy decided to pay his son a surprise, spur-of-the-moment visit. This visit took place in the Boston apartment ML shared with a friend, Philip Lenud.

Daddy cut straight to the chase and pulled no punches. It wasn't that he didn't like Coretta personally. He did. He thought she was a nice young lady. The problem was that at the time ML was dating another woman, whom Daddy quite approved of. All indications were that ML would propose to this young lady. Daddy went so far as to say to Coretta that the other lady "had quite a bit to offer his son." The next words out of her mouth confirmed that Coretta was "my kind of girl." I knew I loved her on the spot. Coretta looked Daddy square in the eye and replied, "You know, I have quite a bit to offer as well."

Needless to say, he got over whatever hesitation he had. From the moment they married, he loved Coretta like a daughter. And she loved him like her own father. They supported each other through all the good times, the hard times, the danger, all the twists and turns of the movement and ultimately through ML's assassination and beyond. They were always there for each other, and there was nothing each would not do for the other—whatever was required.

Coretta was always strong, self-assured, and independent. I remember on another occasion, ML was late picking her up for a date. He sat in the car and blew the horn when he arrived. She took her time and pointedly made him wait. She clearly and effectively communicated that she did not appreciate his tardiness. Again, I knew she was my kind of lady.

Not long after they began seeing each other, ML proposed. To his lasting relief and great joy, Coretta accepted. Once again, he had no money. He wasn't working at the time. I ended up loaning him the money for Coretta's engagement ring.

They were married June 18, 1953, at the home of Obadiah and Bernice Scott, Coretta's parents, in Alabama.

The day of the wedding had a touch of drama, just to keep things interesting.

To begin with, ML had not gotten the marriage license. He delayed and stalled and put it off until he had no alternative. He'd have to get the license that day—the day of his wedding. This didn't sit well with our father at all. Daddy was a stickler for being on time. All that morning, he was on ML for procrastinating. Remember, we were in Atlanta and would commute that morning to Alabama for the wedding. And it was in Alabama that he had to get the license.

Daddy spent the morning yelling through the house, "ML, boy, you're going to be late and it's your own wedding."

Naturally, since ML would have to make a special stop at an Alabama courthouse to pick up the marriage license, Dad thought the rest of us should depart Atlanta for Alabama before ML. Frustrated with him for being so slow, Dad announced at the top of his voice that we would be leaving ahead of ML, which we did, in fact, do. Dad, Mother, and I all left for the drive to Alabama.

To this day, we don't know how ML managed to make the trip in time, get the license, and meet the rest of us at Coretta's parents' home in time for the ceremony.

Once we arrived at the Scott home, Coretta's sister Edythe and I decided to decorate the arch in the yard. The yard was huge, and there was plenty of open space. The nearest neighbor was probably a mile or so away. There were woods near the house, so that's where we went to find decorative flowers. In a matter of moments we found an assortment of beautiful wildflowers that transformed a dull, basic plain arch into a beautiful, eye-catching attraction.

ML AND CORETTA ON THEIR WEDDING DAY. OUR BROTHER, AD, IS
TO ML'S RIGHT AND SERVED AS BEST MAN. I'M TO AD'S RIGHT;
HIS WIFE, NAOMI, IS BETWEEN ML AND CORETTA. MOTHER AND
DADDY ARE TO THE CENTER/RIGHT OF THE PHOTO. CORETTA'S
SISTER EDYTHE AND THEIR PARENTS ARE AT THE RIGHT. THE
FLOWER GIRL IS AD'S DAUGHTER ALVEDA.

Daddy performed the ceremony.

Following the wedding, I stayed overnight with Coretta's parents. ML and Coretta stayed at the home of friends, Mr. and Mrs. Robert E. Tubbs. Coretta drove to the Tubbses' while ML slept on the way. He had, after all, made the drive from Boston to Alabama, with only a brief layover in Atlanta. Then he made that harried drive to Alabama for the marriage license on the day of the wedding.

The next day, the three of us, ML, Coretta, and I, returned to Atlanta. Shortly thereafter, the newlyweds returned to Boston to complete their studies. ML was working on his dissertation and Coretta was wrapping up at the conservatory.

In many ways, this was a period of calm before personal and world-changing events. ML would soon accept the Call of Destiny and become the new pastor of Montgomery's Dexter Avenue Baptist Church. On the horizon awaited his rendezvous with history, Rosa Parks, and the Montgomery Improvement Association.

I have always believed that providence, history, and destiny combined to place my brother at the head of a nonviolent, revolutionary movement that would inspire people the world over to work out the means for their own emancipation from the challenges of racism, war, discrimination, poverty, and oppression.

The seeds ML planted bore fruit from Montgomery, Alabama, to Johannesburg, South Africa. The cheering throngs jubilantly celebrating the collapse of the Berlin Wall sang "We Shall Overcome," the anthem of our movement. We see the genius of his work in the women's movement, the movement for a more "green" environment, the battle against discrimination based on sexual preference, and in human rights campaigns the world over.

ML was on the global stage for an all-too-brief thirteen years—from December 1955, starting in Montgomery, Alabama, with Rosa Parks and the bus boycott, through April 1968 and the striking sanitation workers in Memphis, Tennessee. His impact continues to be felt today in politics, both domestic and international, and in progressive advocacy for social change, wherever people find themselves oppressed and abused.

What follows are my recollections and observations, as I watched my brother grapple with doing what he called "God's will" on so very many occasions.

The headlines and the big stories of Montgomery, Birmingham, the March on Washington, Selma, the Nobel Prize, and his evolving opposition to an "immoral, unjust war in Vietnam" are well known. Fewer people understand his skepticism about the military industrial complex and the ravages of capitalism toward the end of his life. In my opinion, it is these positions—not the oft-cited demand for a seat at the front of the bus, or integration—that led to his assassination.

What is not so well known, however, are the personal tales of these epic struggles; the impact they had on our parents, our family, his wife and children—and what I saw, felt, observed, lived, and breathed as a loving, supportive sister during ML's leadership of the "civil rights movement."

I put that phrase in quotation marks because in some ways it is entirely too limiting. Martin professed a philosophy and a set of nonviolent direct-action tactics and strategies that empowered the "least of these" to remain humble and defeat even the most powerful of adversaries.

Think of the photograph of the lone Chinese protester courageously staring down a column of battle-ready tanks after the massacre in Tiananmen Square.

What follows are the stories of my brother and his movement, from his older sister's perspective.

8

WATCHING ML ANSWER THE CALL
TO DESTINY: MONTGOMERY'S DEXTER
AVENUE BAPTIST CHURCH

*B*y early 1954, America's soil had been tilled and the nation was ripe for change. It was as if there was a cosmic convergence of crucial elements placing the country on the cusp of social revolution. On May 17, the United States Supreme Court handed down its groundbreaking, precedent-shattering decision in the case of *Brown* v. *Topeka Board of Education*, holding the Jim Crow doctrine of "separate but equal" to be inherently unequal, and thus, unconstitutional.

ML and Coretta were finishing up their graduate work in Boston. He completed requirements for his Ph.D., on June 5, 1955, and that spring Coretta also graduated from the New England Conservatory of Music. ML had been told by a family friend, T. M. Alexander, Sr., that Montgomery's Dexter Avenue Baptist Church was seeking a new pastor. Mr. Alexander thought ML was well suited for the position and urged him to apply. As a part of that process, ML delivered an audition sermon titled "Three Dimensions of a

Complete Life." The sermon contemplated the trinity of loving oneself, loving God, and loving one's neighbor. It would later become one of his staple sermons.

Several weeks after delivering this initial sermon, he accepted the call to serve as Dexter's new pastor. At the outset, Coretta was not particularly anxious to return to her home state. However, she eventually came to accept her role as the new, young minister's wife. She realized that in Montgomery they were likely to be tried and tested in ways she could not possibly conceive. Nonetheless, they both believed that the time and place were of God's choosing, and that He had a plan for them and their lives.

With this faith, on the first Sunday in July, Coretta made her first visit to Dexter. ML believed the time had come to introduce her to his new congregation. ML had just turned twenty-five, and Coretta was all of twenty-seven years old.

Dexter was a vibrant, socially active congregation. It had a reputation as "the big people's church." Many of its members were successful businessmen, physicians, college professors, public school teachers, and the like. They were the type of intellectual audience likely to take to ML's thoughtful, reasoned oratory. In this sense, he and this particular church were a wonderful fit.

During this period, ML and Coretta met another young Montgomery minister and his wife—Ralph David and Juanita Abernathy. Reverend Abernathy became one of ML's closest friends, a trusted colleague and a valuable member of the staff of the Southern Christian Leadership Conference. From this point on, he was at ML's side for the battles that would consume the remainder of his life.

Perhaps, as a sign of things yet to come, it's worth noting that the church is just across the street from the Alabama State Capitol, the very building in which the vote to secede from the Union was cast. It is, therefore, not an exaggeration for Montgomery to have been recognized as the "cradle of the Confederacy."

Dexter had been led, to that point, by the Reverend Dr. Vernon Johns, who served from 1947 to 1952. He was a fiery orator, well known for his fierce opposition to segregation as well as for his disdain of elitism among blacks. Dr. Johns hailed from Farmville, a small town in Virginia. He graduated from Oberlin College in 1918 and received his Ph.D. from the University of Chicago's School of Theology.

On Sunday, October 31, 1954, ML was installed as the senior pastor at Dexter, with the Ebenezer Choir on hand for the ceremony. Daddy preached the installation sermon. I led the singing of the anthem "I Will Give Thanks," accompanied by Mother on the organ. Once again, the day had been a King family affair.

Montgomery was a typical southern city with an apparent racial peace. The problem was that this outward calm was secured through the total subjugation and exploitation of the black community. There was not a single black elected official and there were few registered black voters. It was clear to ML and the black community that there existed, beneath Montgomery's public calm, a simmering resentment and suppressed frustration throughout the black community.

At the heart of this milieu was the daily operation of the humiliating, degrading city bus service. There were no black drivers. While courteous white drivers could be found, there were verbally abusive operators as well. It was certainly possible to hear black passengers referred to as "niggers," or worse.

Black riders were required to pay their bus fare at the front door, as anyone would expect.

But, under Montgomery's insane, unique practice, they were required to then get off the bus, only to reboard through the rear door. There were drivers who, after having received the fare, would simply pull away before the passenger could get back on through the rear door. On the bus, the seats at the front were reserved for white passengers. Even if there were no white passengers on the bus, blacks were not allowed to use the seats. Blacks were required to seat from the rear, then proceed forward. If all other seats were full, black passengers had to stand, leaving the "white" seats empty. In the event a white person boarded the bus and there were no more seats left in the white section, black riders in the seats behind the white section had to stand in order that the newly boarded whites could be seated.

Into this scenario, providence thrust itself on December 1, 1955, in the form of Rosa Parks, a respected African American seamstress active in Montgomery's National Association for the Advancement of Colored People (NAACP). As the world now knows, through her courageous act of dignity and resistance, in simply remaining seated when the bus driver demanded that she relinquish her place to a white passenger, Rosa Parks actually took a stand for all that is just and right in terms of the promise of America. Because of her, neither my brother nor America would ever be the same.

E. D. Nixon, president of the state NAACP, learned of Mrs. Parks's arrest for refusing to give up her seat and posted bail. His rage reflected that of the entire community. Local ministers met at the Dexter Avenue Church, where a consensus was reached that Montgomery's black citizens had been subjected to this type of humiliation for far too long. They decided to mount a protest via a one-day boycott of city buses.

The date for the boycott was Monday, December 5, 1955. Over

the intervening weekend, the protester's vision had been given a boost by a bit of unplanned and fortunate publicity. A local newspaper somehow got a copy of a leaflet supporting the boycott and published it on the front page. When Monday finally arrived, the boycott participation rate was close to 100 percent. Buses ran virtually devoid of black passengers the entire day. People hitchhiked, shared rides, and walked—anything rather than further cooperate with the evil of segregation.

The very same day, Mrs. Parks was tried and found guilty of violating the segregation law. This, too, further inflamed the community. It also carried the unintended—yet significant—consequence of reaffirming the justness of the refusal to use the buses. But, more important, because Mrs. Parks's case had not been dismissed as some before hers had been, she was now in a position to appeal the conviction, and the stage was set for a frontal, judicial challenge to the constitutionality of segregation laws.

By that afternoon the ministers decided to create a formal organization to determine how best to proceed. Thus the Montgomery Improvement Association (MIA) was born. ML was elected president. History and hindsight may suggest that he was divinely inspired and placed in Montgomery, specifically to take up this cause. Perhaps this is true, but he was also new in town, already involved in the community, and would be perceived as an ideal candidate for leadership.

A mass meeting was held that evening and the MIA determined to continue the protest until their demands concerning first-come, first-served seating were met. ML spoke, and in so doing, burst onto the stage of history. A new type of leadership was born in the nation that night. He said in part:

There comes a time when people get tired of being trampled over by the iron feet of oppression. There comes a time, my friends, when people get tired of being flung across the abyss of humiliation where they experience the bleakness of nagging despair. There comes a time when people get tired of being pushed out of the glittering sunlight of life's July, and left standing amidst the piercing chill of an Alpine November. We are here this evening because we're tired now.

He then went on to utter the words that would define, control, and guide the remaining thirteen years of his life:

Now let us say that we are not advocating violence. We have overcome that. I want it to be known throughout Montgomery and throughout this nation that we are a Christian people and that the only weapon that we have in our hands this evening is the weapon of protest.

He concluded by saying:

I want it to be known that we're going to work with grim and firm determination to gain justice on the buses in this city. And we are not wrong, we are not wrong in what we are doing. If we are wrong, the Constitution of the United States is wrong. If we are wrong, God Almighty is wrong.

The dawn of the nonviolent civil rights movement was at hand. In hindsight, it's revealing how modest the MIA's initial demands of the bus company were. Black citizens of Montgomery sought only three objectives: courteous treatment by the drivers; first-come, first-served seating, with blacks from the back forward and whites from the front backward; and the hiring of black drivers for majority black routes.

What had begun as a one-day boycott grew into days, weeks, and months. The degree and precision with which the black community organized was a thing of beauty to behold. Car pools, ride sharing, and simple walking became weapons of protest and resistance. In the oppressive environment of Montgomery, this type of bold confrontation of the status quo became, quite simply, unacceptable.

Early in January, during the bus boycott, while ML attended an evening mass meeting, leaving his two-week-old baby daughter Yolanda at home with Coretta, their home was bombed. Yolanda Denise had been born on November 17, 1955. When ML arrived home he discovered a large and angry crowd. Once he knew his family wasn't hurt, he used the opportunity to calm the crowd. Some were armed, all were angry and in no mood to be disrespected and pushed about by the police on the scene. He asked any that had weapons to take them home. He reminded the crowd that the Montgomery movement was based on the fundamental principle of nonviolence. The incident could well have degenerated into bloodshed, rioting, or destruction, but this was prevented by ML's calm, peaceful example and leadership.

As soon as we learned of the bombing, Dad and I drove to Montgomery to be with ML and Coretta. Coretta's parents, likewise, went immediately to be with them. Dad tried to convince them to return with us to Atlanta. Coretta's parents tried to get them to go back to Hieberger with them.

ML refused. He said he had to remain with the people and "could not abandon the movement." Coretta was steadfast. She said her place was beside her husband, and she, too, refused to leave.

The powers-that-be used every tactic available in trying to defeat the boycott. They sought injunctions against the MIA's carpool; they employed old antiboycott laws and indicted leaders and participants of the struggle, ML included. When he was convicted, fined five hundred dollars, and sentenced to 386 days' imprisonment, ML gained even more support nationally. He was becoming well known as the face of the Montgomery struggle. The boycott continued through his trial, conviction, and appeal. The case was eventually heard by the United States Supreme Court. On November 13, 1956, the Court opened a new chapter in American history by finding Alabama's laws requiring segregation by race in public transportation to be unconstitutional. The 381-day boycott was an unqualified success. It demonstrated that segregation was not only a political issue, it was an economic one as well.

ML was recognized as a national leader as a result of the Montgomery victory.

He harnessed the momentum of the event. In February 1957, a new organization based in Atlanta, the Southern Christian Leadership Conference (SCLC), was born. ML was unanimously elected president and served in this capacity until his death. Other changes and growth were also taking place. A second child, Martin Luther King III, was born in Montgomery on October 23, 1957.

In December 1959, ML tendered his resignation to the Dexter Avenue Baptist Church. He accepted Daddy's invitation to return to Atlanta and co-pastor with him at Ebenezer. They were both elated at this new arrangement. It was good to have him and his growing brood back at home with us.

Before ML left Montgomery, Dexter sponsored a farewell reception in his honor. I was accompanied by Isaac at the reception and I took the occasion to inform ML that we were engaged. Upon hearing our news, ML turned to the audience and announced my engagement. It was a wonderful evening, and we prepared for whatever else the future held.

9

BIRMINGHAM: THE STRUGGLE CONTINUES

*I*n the fall of 1958, ML's first book, *Stride Toward Freedom*, was published to excellent reviews. While autographing copies of it in a Harlem store on September 20, he was stabbed by a deranged woman named Izola Curry. Coretta and I traveled to New York that evening with Reverend Ralph Abernathy and friend Bob Williams.

The next morning, we were met by Bayard Rustin, Stanley Levinson, and Ella Baker. By the time we arrived, emergency surgery had already been performed. We found ML resting comfortably at Harlem Hospital, where a doctor informed us just how serious the assault had been. As he put it, the knife's blade had been lodged against ML's aorta, and if he had "merely sneezed," he would not have survived. We were all shaken by the episode, but thankful that he pulled through. Now, after getting through the bombing of ML's home during the bus boycott, we were reminded once more that the price of freedom was high; that it would demand sacrifice and some day could require the ultimate sacrifice of ML's life.

We adjusted to this new reality by resolutely accepting that from here on out the looming specter of death would be a constant presence in our lives. That was just the way it would be. We live in a violent world, and the forces that had degraded, enslaved, and oppressed us since the first Africans set foot on these shores were entrenched. Securing freedom, equality, and first-class citizenship demanded real revolution. A power beyond us all had chosen ML as a guiding force in this revolution. Our role as family, and mine as his sister, was to do all that we could to sustain, comfort, and support him as he "tried to do God's will."

Challenges to racism, discrimination, and segregation were occuring at breakneck speed all across the country. In February 1960, a group of college students in Greensboro, North Carolina, launched the sit-ins. They quietly, respectfully sought service at a Woolworth Department Store lunch counter and were refused. A movement was sparked and it spread like wildfire. In no time, the first few were joined by a torrent, as hundreds of other students came to sit with them, day after day, seeking service.

ML was enthusiastic about the students' activism, and SCLC helped them financially in their organizing efforts. He traveled to North Carolina to meet with a group of students for a dialogue in which he stressed nonviolence. Out of these conversations, the Student Nonviolent Coordinating Committee (SNCC) was born. John Lewis, now a senior member of Congress representing Atlanta, and a civil rights icon in his own right, was one of these new emerging student leaders.

In November 1962, using the straightforward campaign slogan "Segregation Forever," George Wallace was elected Alabama's governor. Birmingham's commissioner of public safety was the infamous Eugene "Bull" Connor. These two men became the major players in the next great battle of the movement: the fight for justice in Birmingham, a town that had been dubbed the most "thoroughly segregated city in America."

Nineteen sixty-three was the year for the centennial observance of the Emancipation Proclamation. In some ways, it seems only appropriate that history placed ML there in Birmingham at the scene of the confrontation that would eventually force a recalcitrant Congress to adopt the Civil Rights Act.

To speak of Birmingham in terms of nonviolence was an oxymoron. It was a violent, dangerous place, with armed citizens, both black and white. It had public servants and Police and Fire departments fully willing to inflict physical harm in the maintenance of white supremacy. There were so many bombings in one neighborhood that it became widely known as "Dynamite Hill." The city itself acquired the nickname "Bombingham." In fact, as ML once pointed out, "There [were] more unsolved bombings of Negro homes and churches in Birmingham than any [other] city in [the] nation."

Reverend Fred Shuttlesworth was a Baptist minister who led the Alabama Christian Movement for Human Rights, an SCLC affiliate and the organization seeking to desegregate Birmingham. His home was among those that were bombed. The task of breaking the back of segregation involved taking on not just public transportation, but the entire racist governing power structure. The city was intransigent and had once gone so far as to shut down public parks and swimming pools rather than integrate them.

ML and SCLC accepted Reverend Shuttlesworth's invitation to join in the Birmingham campaign in early 1963. They were of the opinion that the future course of the nonviolent movement could be significantly defined by a victory there.

Several other defining events occurred during this time. First, in January 1963, ML, Ralph David Abernathy, and Reverend Shuttlesworth met with President John Kennedy and his brother Robert Kennedy, the attorney general. They left dismayed and disappointed after learning that the Kennedy administration, despite the yearning of the community, the success of the movement in other cities, and the long-simmering desire for change across the South, had no plans to introduce progressive civil rights legislation in Congress.

Second, with the election of Albert Boutwell as Birmingham's new mayor, there was a general sense, particularly in the white business community, that the new city leaders should be granted "time" to negotiate and to arrive at a new social arrangement. One of the issues being debated was the removal of "White" and "Colored" signs on water fountains and on public restrooms in downtown stores. At one point, the merchants had come to an informal agreement to remove these daily symbols of degradation, only to be badgered by Bull Connor and other segregationists into reneging. That led to the feeling among white citizens, and most especially in the local religious and business communities, that the continuing protests were "ill-timed and unwise."

Finally, on a more personal note, we were all elated on March 28, 1964, as ML and Coretta welcomed a new member to the family. Their fourth and final child, Elder Bernice Albertine ("Bunny") King, was born in Atlanta. Bernice is now a Spelman graduate, with law and theology degrees from Emory University. When she was born, I helped with cooking, cleaning, taking care of the other kids, and getting to know my new niece. I was glad to do so, and it proved to be a pleasant time before confrontation, conflict, and major events consumed us and the world.

Meanwhile, the Birmingham campaign agreed on four objectives: the upgrading of jobs and the hiring of more blacks in local industries; desegregating facilities in the downtown business district (rest rooms, fitting rooms, lunch counters, water fountains, and the like); appointing a biracial committee for negotiating a plan for desegregating the remainder of the city; and amnesty for arrested demonstrators.

It was the Easter season, and one tactic was to boycott the downtown shopping district. ML spoke to this point when he said at a mass meeting:

> If I were to seek to give you a blueprint for freedom in Birmingham . . . I would say that first, at this moment, we must decide that we will no longer spend our money in businesses that discriminate against us as Negroes.

Again, as was the case several years before in Montgomery, ML and the movement established the link between segregation, discrimination, and economics. There was, indeed, a prosperous economy that profited from discrimination and the mistreatment of an entire class of citizens—the southern black community.

Because it occurred during the Easter shopping season, the boycott proved extraordinarily effective. Downtown businesses were suffering, so much so that Bull Connor sought, and obtained, an injunction halting marches, sit-ins, and other forms of nonviolent, First Amendment–protected peaceful protest. ML decided that his conscience would not allow him to obey an unjust, immoral injunction. He announced that he and Ralph Abernathy would go to jail on Good Friday.

He and the Birmingham community knew the symbolism of this act of faith—and that it would place the city squarely on the front pages of newspapers around the world. It was at this point that a number of Birmingham clergymen published an open letter in the media urging blacks to withdraw support from ML and calling the protests, again, "unwise and untimely."

It was this correspondence that prompted ML to draft, from his cell in solitary confinement, his now famous "Letter from a Birmingham Jail." It was a reasoned, thoughtful, well-articulated thesis that defined, for the world, the moral cause involved in Birmingham, why the city was a crucial site in the battle for freedom, and why the protesters had to follow the dictates of conscience by refusing to wait for a more "opportune time" to confront segregation.

Because he was being held without writing paper, the text of the letter was scribbled in the margins of newspapers and on toilet paper and smuggled out of jail. It was an eloquent dissertation on the entire concept of nonviolent civil disobedience and is recognized in some scholarly circles as one of the greatest examples of persuasive rhetoric produced in the twentieth century.

He said, in part, in reply to the allegation that he was an outsider and not involved in the civic life of Birmingham:

Injustice anywhere is a threat to justice everywhere.

And that:

We are caught in an inescapable network of mutuality, tied in a single garment of destiny.

He continued:

Never again can we afford to live with the narrow, provincial "out-side agitator" idea. Anyone who lives inside the United States can never be considered an outsider anywhere in this country.

In one of the missive's most eloquent passages, ML explained why it was impossible to ask Birmingham's black community to wait for change any longer, and that the issue must be forced, and faced *now*, declaring:

We have waited more than three hundred and forty years for our constitutional and God-given rights. The nations of Asia and Africa are moving with jet-like speed toward the goal of political independence and we still creep at horse and buggy pace toward the gaining of a cup of coffee at a lunch counter. I guess it's easy for those who have never felt the stinging darts of segregation to say "Wait." But when you have seen the vicious mobs lynch your mothers and fathers and drown your sisters and brothers at whim; when you have seen hate filled policemen curse, kick, brutalize, and even kill your black brothers and sisters with impunity; when you see the vast majority of your twenty million Negro brothers smothering in an airtight cage of poverty in the midst of an affluent society . . . when your first name becomes "nigger," your middle name becomes "boy" (however old you are), and your last name becomes "John," and your wife and mother are never given the respected title "Mrs." . . . when you are forever fighting a degenerating sense of "nobodiness," then you will understand why we find it difficult to wait. There comes a time when the cup of endurance runs over, and men are no longer willing to be plunged into an abyss of despair.

The rest of the Birmingham story is now well known. The following week the campaign turned into the "children's crusade" when hundreds of youths of high school age and younger turned out into the streets en masse to join the protests. They literally provided more bodies than the jails could hold. In addition, the scenes of peaceful, nonviolent demonstrators being attacked by snarling police dogs and of their bodies being tossed about by the powerful spray of fire hoses trained on them at the direction of Bull Connor were broadcast worldwide, helping to galvanize public opinion and support for the cause.

At that point, it was only a matter of time until the back of segregation was broken. The U.S. Justice Department stepped up its involvement in negotiations between SCLC, the local affiliates, and the business community. Connor and the segregationists remained intransigent, but the pressure became too great, and eventually a truce agreement to desegregate lunch counters, drinking fountains, fitting rooms, and rest rooms was reached. The settlement included all the movement's objectives, in that all the demonstrators were released from jail and there was an upgrade to the hiring of blacks throughout Birmingham's business sector.

All did not end peacefully, however. Around this time AD's home was bombed. Fortunately, he, Naomi, and their kids were uninjured. That the damage was not more serious was a blessing of God. It turned out that the dynamite charges had been placed in such a way that the force of the explosion was directed outward, away from the home, rather than inward, in which case serious injury or death no doubt would have occurred. We were reminded yet again, as we had been with ML's stabbing, that freedom is not free, and that liberation could demand the ultimate price. We adjusted ourselves to the ever-present danger and accepted the fact that death would always be just around the corner.

We also settled in for the long, hard struggle, in the words of SCLC's slogan, "to redeem the soul of America."

As was often the case, myriad factors combined to shape history.

Unquestionably, the drama of Birmingham dramatized for the nation the plight of black folk living under the Jim Crow laws of the South. Added to that was Governor George Wallace's infamous stand in the schoolhouse door to literally block the desegregation of higher education in Alabama.

President John Kennedy took to the airwaves in response to Wallace's action to announce the submission of the bill that eventually became the Civil Rights Act of 1964.

The president succinctly summarized the impact of Birmingham. He said:

We are confronted primarily with a moral issue. It is as old as the Scriptures and it is as clear as the American Constitution. The heart of the question is whether all Americans are to be afforded equal rights and equal opportunities; whether we are going to treat our fellow Americans as we want to be treated.

He added further:

Now the time has come for this nation to fulfill its promise. The events in Birmingham and elsewhere have so increased the cries for equality that no city or state or legislative body can prudently choose to ignore them.

At the risk of reducing a complex, historical milestone to a cliché, I am left with two distinct feelings. One, the observation that "the rest is history," and the other, my unending sense of pride in the fact that my brothers helped contribute to shaping it.

10

THE MARCH ON WASHINGTON:
ONE OF ML'S FINEST HOURS

*T*he year 1963 was a very good year. And yet, as we found out all too soon, it was likewise, a very bad year. First, the good: There was the victory in Birmingham, and as a result, there was a palpable feeling, a very real sense nationwide, that the flame of freedom was at last beginning to burn a bit more brightly. Countless sit-ins, rallies, demonstrations, and full-scale campaigns for justice were in full swing across the South. The tangible benefit of all these efforts was the desegregation of hundreds of parks, restaurants, swimming pools, lunch counters, and other places that had previously been all but off-limits to black Americans.

After Birmingham, ML's star, as the saying goes, rose. His schedule and the demands on him increased exponentially. He undertook a major speaking tour, which only reinforced in him his conviction that nonviolent direct action and social protest represented the best available tactic for bringing about his constituency's liberation. For years, the principal civil rights leaders and their organizations had broached the idea of staging a major demonstration in Washington, D.C., to place the issues of freedom and equality squarely on the national agenda.

Finally, ML and SCLC, together with SNCC, the NAACP, the National Urban League, the Congress of Racial Equality (CORE), and longtime warrior A. Philip Randolph, founder of the Brotherhood of Sleeping Car Porters, determined the time was at last ripe to pursue the bold vision of the largest nonviolent assembly—ever—to demand civil rights.

They agreed, along with representatives of organized labor, to begin planning the "March On Washington for Jobs and Freedom," the event now known worldwide simply as the March on Washington.

We know now that ML's delivery of the immortal "I Have a Dream" speech on August 28, 1963, was, indeed, one of his finest hours.

Here is part of the personal story behind that epic event.

But first, I am compelled to make the observation that, although the leaders of the march—Roy Wilkins (NAACP), Whitney Young (Urban League), ML (SCLC), James Farmer (CORE), John Lewis (SNCC), and A. Philip Randolph (Brotherhood of Sleeping Car Porters)—have come collectively to be referred to as the "Big Six," there is another name that should forever be enshrined on that list. It belongs to Dorothy Height, the president of the National Conference of Negro Women, a heroine who served in that capacity for years. Truth be told—and I intend to tell it here—the hierarchy of the movement was generally male oriented. This in America, in the 1960s (*imagine that!*). There were, however, for the record, countless women involved in the day-to-day business of the struggle, in the strategizing and certainly in the sacrifice and suffering, many of whom never got their proper acknowledgment. And Dorothy Height is chief among them.

Dr. Height was intimately involved in planning and organizing the march. She was certainly the political and intellectual equal of every man in the room. Moreover, although "retired," she's still out there on the battlefield. The nation most recently saw her in 2007, still at it—even while seated in a wheelchair. A few years ago, she attended and participated in the groundbreaking ceremony for the newly planned memorial to ML on the Mall in Washington, D.C.

One last bit of credit that must be given for the successful outcome of the march must go to the late Bayard Rustin. Bayard was an excellent organizer, and the flawless character of the events surrounding the march is a testament to this fact. He took the lead in coordinating the hundreds of volunteers, the transportation and crowd-control issues, and all the countless other details required to successfully stage one of the greatest witnesses for freedom in American history.

ML traveled to Washington with Coretta the day before the march and ensconced himself in a hotel to finish his speech. He worked on it all day, and all through the night. He was a perfectionist when it came to his sermons, speeches, and public addresses. He worked in longhand on legal pads, turning out draft after draft, incorporating changes, revisions, and edits as he went along.

He was so immersed in preparation, I'm sure, that he hardly knew where the time went. After he had worked all night, the day of the march arrived. Early that morning, Ralph Abernathy and Bayard Rustin came by the hotel to meet ML. Once they knew the crowd was already beginning to gather, they headed out to join the throng.

What is not generally known is that much of the "I Have a Dream" address was totally extemporaneous and ad-libbed. Parts of it had been taken from snippets of other speeches and sermons he'd delivered in the past. But, if you look closely at television footage, you'll see that once ML hits his Baptist minister's cadence, as he gets into the portion describing his dream, he's neither reading nor referring to notes. He was moved and overtaken by the spirit of the moment. Something spiritual, and not of man, was clearly at work. It was a sterling example of the perfect melding of the man and his moment.

He was articulating a vision for what America had yet to deliver on behalf of its black citizens in order to more fully realize the democratic ideals originally envisioned by the Founding Fathers. He was swept up, and we all knew, right along with him, that he was articulating a vision for the ages.

Oddly enough, neither my parents nor I witnessed the "I Have a Dream" speech in person. Daddy and Mother didn't feel up to traveling and decided against flying to Washington. I was sick with a virus and flulike symptoms. We stayed in Atlanta and watched it on the television in my parents' family room, just like millions of other awestruck Americans. I remember marveling at what an excellent job ML had done. I specifically remember being aware of the precise moment at which he departed from the prepared text. I was totally in synch with him when he began speaking directly from his heart. I also remember the lump rising in my throat when he intoned:

> *Let freedom ring from the prodigious hilltops of New Hampshire . . .*
> *let freedom ring from the snow-capped mountains of Colorado . . .*
> *let freedom ring from Stone Mountain of Georgia; let freedom ring*

*from Lookout Mountain of Tennessee; let freedom ring from every
hill and molehill of Mississippi. From every mountainside, let freedom ring.*

We sat there in stunned and absolute silence. You could have
heard a pin drop. We were so proud we didn't know what to do or
say. And our pride was not just for ML, who had so completely
seized the moment. We were well aware that we had just watched as
my brother's speech took its place alongside the greatest political
orations in the nation's history. We also knew full well that ML had
framed the hopes and aspirations of an entire movement and placed
them squarely at the center of America's consciousness—and that
of the rest of the world.

The other thing I clearly remember is that at the moment he
got the last word out of his mouth and stepped away from the podium, the telephone began to ring instantly and incessantly with
calls of congratulations from church members, friends, and neighbors.

What an incredible, unforgettable moment in my life!

I guess there's one other fact I'd like to share about the march.
For years, people have wondered who the men in the white caps
standing behind ML as he spoke were. The answer, at long last, is
that they were members of the Bakers Union who had volunteered
to provide security that day.

As so often seemed the case, it felt as if, for every moment of
great exultation and joy, there was an equal period of pain and despair. That proved to be the case for both the remainder of 1963
and the weeks immediately following the march.

After the enormous triumph in Washington, a scant eighteen

days later, on Sunday, September 15, we all experienced the devastating impact of the bombing of Birmingham's Sixteenth Street Baptist Church. The story of the vile, senseless murder of four little girls in their Sunday School finest is now well known. ML, like all right-thinking Americans, seethed with frustration and anger. He complained that the atmosphere that allowed such an act was a direct consequence of the unyielding adherence to segregation of so many southern politicians. He delivered the eulogy for three of the girls who died, and he said specifically that their murders stood as "blood on the hands of Governor George Wallace."

And finally, on November 22, there was the assassination of President John F. Kennedy. While watching television news reports from Dallas, ML turned to Coretta and somberly, prophetically remarked, "That's going to happen to me, too."

TRAVEL TO NORWAY AND THE
CELEBRATION OF ML'S NOBEL PEACE PRIZE

*A*s had been the case the preceding year, 1964 proved to be a simultaneous example of the best of times and the worst of times.

In early January, *Time* magazine designated ML its Man of the Year.

It was also the year that saw President Lyndon Johnson achieve a major legislative and political victory as he shepherded the Civil Rights Act through a tepid Congress and achieved its passage.

And then, on December 10, in a magnificent ceremony in Oslo, Norway, ML was awarded the Nobel Prize for Peace. He became the award's third black recipient, and, at age thirty-five, the youngest recipient ever.

Ironically, he received word of his selection while flat on his back, as a patient at Saint Joseph's Hospital in Atlanta, where he had been temporarily hospitalized for treatment of exhaustion. Coretta telephoned him to inform him that she'd been notified of his selection by the Nobel committee.

THIS FAMOUS PHOTO IS ONE OF MY FAVORITES. IT SHOWS MOTHER, DADDY, AD, CORETTA, AND ME SURROUNDING ML AFTER THE CEREMONY IN WHICH HE RECEIVED THE NOBEL PRIZE.

Clearly, the committee's decision recognized the success of his efforts in the Montgomery bus boycott, the battle of Birmingham, and the March on Washington. The much deeper meaning, of course, was that the award bestowed worldwide recognition on ML's leadership and confered the stamp of international approval and legitimacy on the nonviolent struggle for civil rights.

This should have been one of the happiest moments in his life. But that's not the way it played out. Far from it, in fact.

Incensed that ML had been chosen for the Nobel Prize, FBI director J. Edgar Hoover, a determined opponent of the movement and a man who held personal animosity and contempt for ML, had called a press conference specifically to declare him "the most notorious liar in the country."

This statement was made with ML having full knowledge of the fact that the FBI had him under intense, continual observation. Around this time, Atlanta police chief Herbert Jenkins had come to Daddy and warned him to "tell his son to be careful, because he'd been placed under surveillance." He added, "They even know when he goes to the bathroom."

The combined effect of Hoover's statement and his personal knowledge of the FBI's surveillance was a considerable dampening of ML's spirit during the journey to Norway for the presentation ceremony. At a time when he should have been at his emotional apex, he was troubled and distracted by Hoover's rant. He was immensely concerned over what would come next from Hoover's bag of dirty tricks. It's no secret that Hoover was committed to destroying ML's reputation and frustrating the movement in any way he could. The "notorious liar" comment was just one in a string of efforts to sabotage ML's leadership, evidenced most clearly by the

COINTELPRO intelligence surveillance program directed against ML and other black leaders.

As declassified documents and congressionally obtained evidence disclosed in the 1970s, the FBI conducted a long-running, well-organized surveillance campaign designed to neutralize, frustrate, and slander the civil rights movement and its leaders. The full collection of assorted tactics came together under the heading COINTELPRO—short for Counter Intelligence Program.

It was not just ML and SCLC that were victims of these systematic governmental abuses; countless progressive movements across the nation were targets as well, the Black Panther Party prominent among them. In many cases, undercover operatives were introduced into the organizations to foment discord and discontent among the membership. The FBI's tactics also included outright spying, communication intercepts via wiretaps and "bugs," constant surveillance, and an all-out effort to poison the political environment in which the civil rights movement operated.

The man-hours and resources devoted to ML and SCLC during this time far exceeded the attention given to this country's most wanted mobsters. During this period some members of the Black Panther Party, the Weather Underground, Students for a Democratic Society, and similar organizations were driven to hide out with friends, relatives, or fellow cell members in the United States for years. Others sought shelter and santuary in places as varied as Cuba and Algeria. In one case, a suburban soccer mother was able to blend into a well-heeled Minneapolis community for years under an assumed name.

It is truly ironic that ML, one of today's most celebrated Americans, was at one time America's most scrutinized citizen. This observation becomes even more ironic and instructive when one considers this all preceeded the issues with which we are currently confronted, with the Homeland Security apparatus and the Patriot Act, these many years later.

We put together quite a traveling party for the trip to Oslo to receive the prize. Naturally, this did not happen without sacrifice and expense. One Sunday after church, ML called mother and me into his office at Ebenezer, where he informed us he had contacted some of his friends in the ministry, asking if they could help defray the costs of taking his parents and family to Norway for the ceremony. These friends proved more than happy to be of assistance, and they responded generously to ML's appeal.

MOTHER, DADDY, CORETTA, AND I BOARD THE FLIGHT BOUND FOR OSLO, NORWAY, TO WITNESS ML RECEIVING THE NOBEL PEACE PRIZE.

The full delegation that made the trip to witness ML receiving the Nobel Peace prize, consisted of Coretta, Mother, Daddy, AD, and myself, joined by Ralph and Juanita Abernathy, Andy Young, ML's personal secretary Dora McDonald, Dorothy Cotton, O. M. Hoover, with his daughter Carol Hoover, and Freddye Henderson, the owner of an Atlanta black business institution, Henderson's Travel Service, which arranged the trip.

Before the trip, Mrs. Henderson made a suggestion that gave us all pause. She correctly pointed out that it generally wasn't wise for

THE ENTIRE TRAVELING PARTY FOR THE JOURNEY TO OSLO, NORWAY. AT MRS. FREDDYE HENDERSON'S VERY WISE SUGGESTION, WE SPLIT INTO TWO GROUPS SO AS NOT TO ALL BE ON THE SAME FLIGHT. AMONG THOSE SHOWN HERE ARE ML AND CORETTA, MOTHER AND DAD, AD, BAYARD RUSTIN, L. D. REDDICK, HARRY AND LUCY WACHTEL, CHANCEY ESKRIDGE, DORA MCDONALD, DOROTHY COTTON, DR. AND MRS. RALPH ABERNATHY, MARIAN LOGAN, NINA MILLER, REVEREND ANDREW YOUNG, REVEREND O. M. HOOVER, CAROL HOOVER, AND SEPTIMA CLARK.

an entire family to fly together. After some thought, it made sense, and we accepted the logic behind it. Nonetheless, it's one of those things that makes you pause and think. We followed her suggestion and broke up into two smaller traveling parties that were booked on separate flights.

Before reaching Oslo, we stopped in London, where ML preached at the magnificent seventeenth-century St. Paul's Cathedral. I remember the angelic voices of the choir, composed exclusively of men and boys, all of whom sang soprano, as they echoed off the stone and marble walls of the church. And I remember the church's striking architecture and façade.

The Nobel ceremony, held in Aula Hall at Oslo University, was grand, quite formal, and conducted in accordance with strict and rigid protocol. The committee had been in constant contact with Dora McDonald as they explained protocol and worked out details for the trip and our itinerary. We were all assigned specific seats for the ceremony and in the cars that transported us to the hall, which was no more than three or four blocks from the hotel. The king of Norway sat in an aisle near us, and I remember that the doors to the hall were closed at a specific time, and that no one would be allowed entry after the king's arrival. The chair of the Nobel Committee, Dr. Gunnar Jahn, presented the medal and scroll to ML, who then said:

I am mindful that only yesterday in Birmingham, Alabama, our children, crying out for brotherhood, were answered with fire hoses, snarling dogs, and even death. I am mindful that only yesterday in Philadelphia, Mississippi, young people seeking to secure the right to vote were brutalized and murdered. Therefore I must ask why this prize is awarded to a movement which is beleaguered and commit-

ted to unrelenting struggle; to a movement which has not won the very peace and brotherhood which is the essence of the Nobel Prize. After contemplation I conclude that this award, which I receive on behalf of the movement, is a profound recognition that nonviolence is the answer to the crucial political and racial questions of our time—the need for man to overcome oppression without resorting to violence.

He concluded by sharing his upbeat, optimistic point of view, declaring that:

I accept this award today with an abiding faith in America and an audacious faith in mankind. I refuse to accept the idea that man is mere flotsam and jetsam in the river which surrounds him. I refuse to accept the view that mankind is so tragically bound to the starless midnight of racism and war that the bright daylight of peace and brotherhood can never become a reality.

Those few words capture the essence of who my brother was, and what his life, and the eventual sacrifice of it, were all about.

During the trip, both my parents had their moments. I remember Mother Dear, her heart full, while accompanying her firstborn son, fiddling and fussing as she helped him get the knot in his tie, and his formal morning suit "just right." And, as long as I live, I will never forget Daddy's pride in ML's accomplishment. Here was a man, a sharecropper's son from Stockbridge, Georgia, watching his son receive one of the world's greatest humanitarian honors. He was simply overjoyed, and the tears flowed freely and unashamedly during the ceremony.

There's another incident from the trip that I recall fondly. After the ceremony we went back to the hotel, where we had a small, intimate celebration for family and friends. The champagne flowed. A round of toasts was made. And then, we got to Daddy—a teetotaler—who was so taken by the moment that he shouted that he "just wanted to toast God" for allowing us to live to see the occasion.

We spent several days in Oslo, and then traveled to Stockholm, where the bestowing of the other Nobel Prizes, in fields like science and medicine, took place. There's a final lighthearted memory from this period that I should like to share. In Stockholm, there was a reception to honor all the other Nobel laureates. A group of us, Andy Young, Dora McDonald and I, arrived at the venue early, well ahead of other guests. There was a band rehearsing and warming up in preparation for the event. We were all giddy about the week's events and took to the dance floor while the band played. In short order, we were approached by representatives of the Nobel Committee, who reminded us, in no uncertain terms, of the strict protocols involved in all aspects of the Nobel experience. We were quietly but firmly made aware that this spontaneous celebration and dancing was frowned upon.

The conversation was much too direct to be considered a hint, but we got the point. We ceased our prereception revelry and waited for the remainder of the guests before dancing to our hearts' content, in celebration of ML, "Tweed," from the Old Fourth Ward of Atlanta, Georgia, my younger brother, recipient of the 1964 Nobel Peace Prize.

By week's end, we were thoroughly exhausted, and I, for one, was not looking forward to the long flight back to home. Our return to Atlanta was at least broken by a brief stop in New York. At the request of Daddy's friend Governor Nelson Rockefeller we attended a reception for ML at the 369th Regimental Armory, which Governor Rockefeller organized. In addition, while we were in town, New York mayor Robert Wagner presented ML with a key to the city. We all attended the reception, and like everything else associated with the Nobel Prize trip, it was a grand affair.

What we didn't know was that back home in Atlanta quite a controversy was brewing. The progressives in the civic community, who always viewed Atlanta as the standard bearer for the "New South," felt the city should formally recognize its native son on his receipt of the Nobel Prize. To that end, some business leaders proposed hosting a dinner in ML's honor. That proposal was greeted with resistance and opposition by those in the business community still committed to maintaining the old southern way of doing things. Finally, because of the intervention and insistence of Mayor Ivan Allen and Robert Woodruff, philanthropist and chairman of the Coca-Cola Company, an appropriate sold-out, jam-packed dinner was held at the Downtown Dinkler Plaza Hotel. Nobel Prize winner and native Atlantan Martin Luther King, Jr., had finally received the accolades of his hometown.

SELMA AND THE STRUGGLE
FOR THE RIGHT TO VOTE

*E*ven with the victories in Montgomery and in Birmingham, even with the success of the March on Washington, and even in the afterglow of ML's receipt of the Nobel Peace Prize, there remained work to be done. The year was 1965, and there still existed an immense void in the struggle for African Americans to secure the status and trappings of first-class citizenship: securing federal protection for the right to vote.

The field on which that epic confrontation would be waged was Selma, Alabama, and for good reason: In the early 1960s roughly 57 percent of Selma's population was black. There were fifteen thousand voting-age black citizens, yet only 130 were actually on the rolls as registered voters. At one point, a group of thirty-two black teachers attempted to register to vote. All were promptly fired by the all-white school board.

ML believed the highest expression of black Americans' new-found gains must come in the polling places. He had said for years, "If you give us the ballot, we will elect men of good will to the legislatures." With the explosion of black elected officials, the growth of the Congressional Black Caucus, and in an era in which black Americans compete for and serve in the highest offices in the land, I can't help but feel that ML's efforts to secure the right to free exercise of the ballot have been vindicated.

NOT ALL THE WORK OF THE MOVEMENT WAS DONE IN SUITS AND TIES. HERE, ML, AD, AND C. T. VIVIAN AND BERNARD LEE ARE SHOWN IN A HOTEL ROOM IN A PHOTO FROM A 1965 *JET* MAGAZINE STORY, MAKING PLANS AND STRATEGIZING FOR THE SELMA CAMPAIGN.

Just as Birmingham had been the flashpoint that produced the Civil Rights Act of 1964, it was Selma's destiny to be the cauldron in which the Voting Rights Act was forged.

ML told his followers they'd have to be prepared to go to jail by the thousands in order to secure the right to vote. He went on to say, "We are not asking . . . we are *demanding* the ballot."

As is now well known, plans were made to mount a fifty-four-mile march from Selma to the State capitol in Montgomery to dramatize the demand for unfettered access to the ballot.

In those days, we must remember, not just in Alabama, but across the length and breadth of the South, literacy tests, poll taxes, grandfather clauses, and many other types of creative subterfuge were employed to keep black men and women from registering to vote. Therefore, there was a need for federal legislation that would remove these barriers and foster an environment in which citizens could freely participate in the highest calling of a democracy: registering and casting an equal vote on the major issues and candidates of the day.

People have remarked that they don't often see pictures of me at marches and other events. I was there, but the truth is, I've never been one for high-profile participation. However, I always tried to be there to help provide attention to detail, and to do the small things necessary to make whatever project ML and his staff were engaged in flow a bit more smoothly.

The Selma campaign was somewhat different. ML asked that I sing at the opening rally on the day we departed for Montgomery. Of course, I complied. So I was there in Selma, at his request, and took to the podium to lead in the singing of the Star Spangled Banner. ML was always a patriot, and this song selection certainly set the right tone for the march that was about to get underway.

There was a large crowd, all fully prepared to undertake the trek to Montgomery and dedicated to helping secure access to the ballot. They were, in actuality, preparing to set out across the Black Belt of Alabama to make the promise of American democracy real to hundreds of thousands of black citizens trapped behind the "cotton curtain."

I am reminded of another instance of my personal participation. Several years earlier, in 1962, James Meredith, the black student who desegregated the University of Mississippi, had undertaken his "March Against Fear." His intent was to march across the state of Mississippi without the benefit of huge throngs of supporters or massive coverage by the press. Only a day or so into the march, Meredith was leveled by a shotgun blast fired from the nearby woods. Luckily, he survived, and his wounds were not serious.

ML and others felt an obligation to help complete the "Meredith March." This sense of obligation was both moral and practical. Morally, there was the need to support Mr. Meredith and to make a profound statement by refusing to be intimidated, and to complete the march.

Practically, there was the need to illustrate that the movement could not be sidetracked by simply murdering protesters any time a challenge to the status quo was mounted. A consensus was reached that a clear and unequivocal example of the determination to be free was crucial.

Thus, the decision to take up the march from the site of the shooting. I, too, made up my mind that I had to be there and participate.

Now, I must confess to my own naïveté. I wasn't prepared with the proper footwear for a march along a Mississippi blacktop highway. Rather than wearing boots or sneakers, I showed up in a pair of summer sandals.

Big mistake.

Early on, someone behind me stepped on my heel. I can't begin to describe the pain.

Being stepped on wasn't so bad—but mile after mile of picking my foot up and laying it down was pure torture. By the time I returned home and was ready to get off the plane, my foot was so swollen I could barely walk. My foot and heel throbbed with every single step. It was awful.

There's no need to recount the events of the Selma campaign in great detail here. What the world witnessed on the Edmund Pettus Bridge on "Bloody Sunday," March 7, 1965, speaks for itself, as it has for the ensuing four decades.

As newsreels and documentaries show, a force of Alabama state troopers, many mounted on horseback, charged into a column of peaceful, nonviolent protesters led by John Lewis and Hosea Williams, one of SCLC's most brilliant organizers and a longtime close aide to ML. Tear gas canisters were fired, marchers were maced and billyclubbed, and a number were run over by horses. The carnage was among the most horrific of the movement.

It became clear a few days later that the tide of history was preparing to sweep up the state of Alabama and spew forth a new era of black participation in southern and national politics. A federal Voting Rights Act was on the horizon. The die was unalterably cast when President Lyndon Johnson went on nationwide television to tell America:

> *At times history and fate meet at single time in a single place to shape a turning point in man's unending search for freedom. So it was a century ago at Appomattox. So it was last week in Selma, Alabama.*
>
> *What happened in Selma is part of a far larger movement which reaches into every section and state of America. It is the effort of American Negroes to secure for themselves the full blessings of American life. . . . It's not just Negroes, but all of us, who must overcome the crippling legacy of bigotry and injustice . . . and we shall overcome.*

Two weeks after the bloodshed on the Pettus Bridge, ML led a triumphant crowd of over three thousand onto the grounds of the state capitol in Montgomery, where he engaged in a rhetorical call and response. "How long? Not long . . . no lie can live forever," he said. "Truth crushed to earth shall rise again," he declared.

Once again, my brother had been engaged in changing the course of history. The electoral face of the South and the nation as a whole was about to undergo a metamorphosis of revolutionary proportions.

On August 6, 1965, Lyndon Johnson signed the Voting Rights Act into law. As a memento of the occasion, he gave ML one of the pens he used in signing the legislation. It became a treasured keepsake.

My mother had a sibling who died as a child.

He was her brother, named Parks Williams. She often recalled him and his loss with particular fondness, and yet with a sense of melancholy nostalgia, in stories she shared with me during my childhood. What she recalled most vividly was Parks's funeral and the ride to the gravesite at Atlanta's Southview Cemetery, the site of the final resting places for the majority of the King family.

As she told the story, they made their way to the cemetery in a horse-drawn carriage. Her brother's tiny coffin was wedged between her parents, A. D. Williams and Jennie Celeste Williams. She told me that what she recalled most clearly was the mournful sound of the horse's hooves as they rhythmically scraped against the pavement while they solemnly made their way along the funeral route.

The weather that day was dark and gray. A misty rain fell as the family gathered around the freshly dug grave without the protection of umbrellas or other shelter.

In her own little-girl way, my mother wondered why they were leaving her brother in the cold, wet Georgia earth. She pondered over whether she would ever see him again.

I have always marveled at the way the human mind works, and at how same stories stick out in our consciousness—at the way Mother Dear, for example, retained this story, and at the way I have kept it fresh in my mind for all these many years.

I suppose, subconsciously, I've wondered whether this tale represented some type of precursor for what lay ahead for our family in terms of death, life, and grief. God knows, funerals have played a significant role in the story of the King family.

What follows are my personal recollections of trying times of loss, grief, and pain, and the ways we tried to keep on going when there seemed to be such hopelessness and despair.

And in some ways, this, too, is a story of perseverance, redemption, and grace.

It is the tale of how I have tried to be true to Daddy's admonition when his grandchildren—in pain from Mother's murder, as she played the Lord's Prayer at Ebenezer one Sunday morning—questioned why these terrible things continued to happen to our family.

Daddy replied simply, "I know it's hard to understand, but we have to give thanks for what we have left. God wants us to love one another and not hate."

I have spent much of my adult life trying to live up to the example Daddy set for us on that day.

13

LOSING ML IN MEMPHIS

At the point the Voting Rights Act became law, I believe that a major phase of ML's life came to an end. From 1955 and the Montgomery bus boycott through 1965 and Selma's realization of the protections of the Voting Rights Act, he'd been involved in dismantling the last vestiges of the overt Jim Crow South: segregated public accommodations, the refusal of service at lunch counters, being relegated to the balcony in movie theaters, confinement to the back of the bus, and so forth.

During this period, it seems to me, ML believed and attempted to prove that an appeal to the moral conscience of America could bring black people into the mainstream of this society.

I'm also convinced that something else equally significant soon occurred: He underwent profound spiritual, political, and intellectual growth. Some commentators have described it as his having taken on a more militant tone. But that's far too simplistic an explanation. What really occurred is that he expanded his focus and developed a broader worldview, which would, in turn, dominate the remainder of his days. His thinking evolved and he began to see the system itself was fundamentally flawed and in need of radical restructuring.

It is also my belief that many contemporary scholars and historians fail to grasp the depth of ML's revolutionary philosophical and analytical shift in the years between 1965 and 1968.

Far too often, popular culture appears intent on sanitizing him. At times, there seems to be a concerted effort to cast him as simply a nonthreatening, idle dreamer and pacifist concerned only with questions of integration and civil rights.

In my opinion no characterization could be further from the truth or more historically inaccurate.

He said it far better than I can, when he declared:

> *If we are to get on the right side of the world revolution we as a nation must undergo a radical revolution of values. We must rapidly begin the shift from a "thing-oriented" society to a "people-oriented" society. When machines and computers are considered more important than people, the giant evil triplets of racism, materialism, and militarism are incapable of being conquered.*

During this period he began to pose uncomfortable questions about capitalism and exploitation of the poor. To the dismay of many who had been staunch allies—until then—he spoke out on the "unjust, immoral war in Vietnam."

With this new, enhanced world perspective, he made the connection between colonialism, racism, and economic exploitation in the Third World. He began to associate the struggle for civil rights here with battles for human rights and with national liberation movements in Africa, Asia, and Latin America.

I say all of this because it is essential to viewing in proper context the ML who went to Memphis, Tennessee, in the spring of 1968; the ML who continued to be driven by "the fierce urgency of now."

In April, ML was in the middle of planning for the Poor People's Campaign—a mass movement envisioned by SCLC to physically take poor people from across the nation to Washington, D.C., to lobby Congress for economic justice and, among other things, a guaranteed national income. In the midst of this he received a call from a longtime friend, the Reverend James Lawson, asking him to lend his support to Memphis sanitation workers who had gone on strike for higher wages and safer working conditions.

As I noted, ML had become increasingly concerned with militarism, racism, and poverty, particularly the exploitation of the poor. He saw what was happening in Memphis as a perfect illustration of this exploitation at work.

As an example of his solidarity with workers, he said to the Memphis strikers:

> *You are demanding that this city will respect the dignity of labor. So often we overlook the work and the significance of those who are not in professional jobs, of those who are not in the so-called big jobs. But let me say to you tonight that wherever you are engaged in work that serves humanity and is for the building of humanity, it has dignity and it has worth.*

We know the story from here On the night of April 3, ML went to the Mason Temple AME Church and delivered his final address. In his "Mountaintop" speech, he said difficult days "were ahead, and that no one really [knew] what would happen next."

He clearly and defiantly declared to the world, "I'm happy to-night; I'm not fearing *any* man."

I'm convinced in my heart that, just as he said, he left that church and went out into the night prepared "to do God's will."

And then—April 4, 1968, one of the worst days of my life. I remember specific portions of it as if it was yesterday; other portions, though, are lost in a conflicting jumble of confusion, emotions, and dread. But above all else, I am forever left with the sensations of shock, horror, pain, and disbelief, and the feeling of being absolutely distraught to the core of my being.

These are the emotions that remain with me to this day—forty years later.

April is, of course, the Easter season. It was a rainy evening, and I was at home on the sewing machine making an Easter dress for Angela. The television was tuned to NBC's nightly *Huntley/Brinkley Report*, when there was a flash that ML had been shot in Memphis.

Obviously, I was scared to death and wanted to know more. I needed to find out as much as I could, as quickly as I could. I began trying to reach my parents by telephone. This was before call waiting, and no matter how many times I dialed Daddy and Mother, I got a busy signal. I was unable to contact them. I was nervous, scared, and frustrated, all at once.

Isaac immediately said, "We've got to go to Coretta's." So we got a neighbor to babysit and quickly set out for ML's home on Sunset Avenue. I was so full of grief and worry that the ride is pretty much a blur. What I remember thinking about was the latest update I'd heard on the news before we left home. Chet Huntley had come back on the air with another bulletin, confirming the shooting and saying ML's condition was "critical." In my mind, critical always meant almost dead.

As we arrived at Coretta's, she was walking out of the door to the driveway, accompanied by Mayor Ivan Allen, Jr. She told us she had been called by Jesse Jackson, who told her she needed "to catch the next thing smoking to Memphis." She asked us to join them as they were on the way to the airport.

I resisted feebly, since I certainly wasn't prepared to travel. I definitely wasn't dressed appropriately to go anywhere. All I was wearing was the housedress I'd had on at home, as I was working on Angela's dress. I wore a raincoat over it. But Isaac again correctly insisted that we go, and that I accompany Coretta to Memphis. We rode to the airport in a police car.

The mayor sat in the front on the passenger side. Isaac and I were in the back, seated on either side of Coretta; we held her hands the entire way. I don't remember talking much as we made our way to the airport. We all, I'm sure, just offered up silent prayers as we watched the raindrops cascading down the windshield. Mayor Allen spent the ride on the police radio trying to gather more information. I still had not been able to reach my parents.

All I can do is reiterate the emotional state I was in: Distraught, confused, worried, and numb with shock is the only way to describe my state of mind.

When we arrived at the airport, we were met by Dora McDonald, ML's secretary, who handed us tickets for a flight to Memphis. To this day I don't know how she took care of those details, or when, or how she purchased the tickets.

Shortly after getting to the airport, I tried contacting my parents, yet again. Once more, I had no luck. I even tried placing an emergency phone call. This, too, proved unsuccessful. I later learned that AD had accompanied ML to Memphis. He had called my parents and was updating them as the evening wore on, which was the reason I was unable to reach Mother and Daddy.

At some point in all the confusion, I saw Dora beckon to Coretta, and they walked into a nearby ladies' room. I quickly went to join them.

Almost instantly, there was a feeble, polite tap on the door. We were joined by a sullen, ashen-faced Mayor Allen, who said in a very formal manner, "Mrs. King, it is my sad duty to inform you that Dr. King has died."

That's how I learned of my brother's assassination—in a bathroom at the Atlanta airport.

Coretta took a moment to absorb the news, as did we all. The first thing out of her mouth, however, was care and concern for her children. She said, "I can't go to Memphis—I have to go home to the children."

That's exactly what we did; we piled back into the police car and returned to their home. An enormous task lay ahead. We had to comfort the children and find a way to begin planning, what remains the largest funeral the city of Atlanta has ever seen.

As we mounted the steps, someone opened the door and told us President Johnson was on the phone. He conveyed condolences to Coretta on behalf of himself, Mrs. Johnson, and the nation. He then told Coretta he was preparing to address the country on live television later that evening.

As we gathered around the television to watch the president's address, we were distracted by the constant ringing of the telephone. One of those calls was from Robert Kennedy, who by then represented the state of New York in the Senate. He had three telephone lines installed, anticipating the deluge of calls that would follow in the coming days. More important, he graciously offered the use of his private plane when he learned of Coretta's plans to go to Memphis the next day to retrieve ML's body.

Harry Belafonte was among the callers that night. He arrived in Atlanta the next day and offered his steadying presence and support to all of us. Harry spent time selecting the tie that would match the suit in which Martin would be buried.

After watching the president's address, Coretta, Dora, and I found ourselves in the bedroom, trying to sort out all that had to be done in planning the funeral. We felt overwhelmed with grief and frustration over the enormous task ahead of us. We knew there had to be music and we began to think about the selections. We knew there would be dignitaries arriving from across the globe and we tried to think about how to organize and prepare for them.

Then, it came to me. I said to Coretta, "You know ML has already preached his own eulogy." Exactly two months earlier, on February 4, at Ebenezer, ML had delivered a sermon entitled "The Drum Major Instinct." In it, he had contemplated his own death—and he even discussed what he'd like to have said at his funeral. Coretta wasn't at church that day, so she hadn't heard it.

SCLC had a weekly program broadcast on black radio stations called *Martin Luther King, Jr., Speaks,* which featured sermons, speeches, and other addresses by ML. We contacted the station in New York that produced the show and had them send us a copy of the tape.

We had it played at the funeral. Absolutely nobody could have done a better job in eulogizing ML than he did himself. He spoke about what he'd like said:

> *I'd like somebody to mention that day that Martin Luther King, Jr., tried to give his life serving others. I'd like for somebody to say that day that Martin Luther King, Jr., tried to love somebody. I want you to say that day that I tried to be right on the war question. . . . I want you to say that I tried to love and serve humanity. And. . . .*
>
> *Yes, if you want to say that I was a drum major, say that I was a drum major for justice. Say that I was a drum major for peace. I was a drum major for righteousness. And all the other shallow things will not matter.*
>
> *I won't have any money to leave behind, I won't have the fine and luxurious things of life to leave behind. But I just want to leave a committed life behind.*
>
> *And that's all I want to say!*

Well past one o'clock in the morning, I finally reached my parent's house. I was amazed because Mother didn't seem to have been crying. She was on the lower level and was immersed in preparing food. I suppose she was just trying to keep busy and keep her mind off what had transpired. We didn't speak . . . all was silent. It was a surreal scene, and I stayed with her for what seemed like hours.

It was quite late when I left my folks' house and headed the few blocks home. It felt like that couple of blocks took forever. It seemed as if everything was moving in slow motion. My only conscious thought was the realization that our world had been irrevocably and forever changed.

The next morning, Senator Kennedy did exactly as he had promised. His plane was waiting for us as a small group gathered for the trip to bring ML home. He also assigned a young black staffer to assist us. His name was Earl Graves, and he went on to become the founder and editor of *Black Enterprise* magazine. Our group included Coretta and me, Jean Young, Andy's wife, Juanita Abernathy, Dora McDonald, Reverend Fred Bennett, a long-time SCLC staffer, and a few others.

I have not returned to Memphis in the forty years since that day. The memories are just too strong and depressing, especially the snapshot I have in my mind after we landed. We never got off the plane. ML's casket was placed in the back and we were joined on board by AD and the SCLC staff who had been there with ML: Ralph Abernathy, Andy Young, James Orange, and Hosea Williams. They were all as exhausted and in as much pain as we were. I'm sure they had been up all night, and probably never left ML's side.

There was a small crowd of ordinary citizens, probably including some of the strikers. They had come to the airport to see us off and to pay their respects. Just as it had been in Atlanta the day before, it was a dark, gloomy, overcast day.

What I can never forget is the security presence. I felt then, and believe now, that it was over the top and uncalled for. The National Guard had been called out and a contingent was there at the airport. They took up positions across from the somber crowd of mourners. They stood there, unflinching, with their bayonets fixed and trained on the people.

The mourners were there purely out of respect for my brother, and they were as torn up and in as much pain as we were. They represented no threat to us. They posed no security risk, and it was obvious they intended no harm. I have never been able to grasp why the military thought such an intimidating presence was called for. It was shameful. I have *never* witnessed anything like it, before or since. These people had tears in their eyes. And we recognized then that ML belonged to them as much as he did to us.

As we left Memphis and returned to Atlanta, all sorts of thoughts rushed through my mind. How would my parents survive the loss of their child? What about Coretta and the children—and what was to become of our country? What would become of the movement and the dreams it encompassed?

When we got back home, ML was taken directly to Hanley's Funeral Home on Auburn Avenue, under a heavy police escort. The weather was still bleak and dreary. It was as if heaven itself was weeping. It was a thoroughly depressing experience that felt as if it dragged on forever. There were no blaring sirens. Just the hush that accompanied the still of silent, flashing red and blue lights.

After we got to Hanley's, I didn't initially want to see ML as the temporary casket was opened. Isaac insisted that I should. Once again, he was right, and I'm glad I relented. Had I not, I'm not sure I would ever have forgiven myself. He looked so calm and at peace. It's become a cliché, but he looked as if he was merely sleeping.

I still stand in awe of Coretta's quiet dignity and strength. Even in the loss of her husband, and the father of her children, she was a paragon of pride and quiet determination. She returned to Memphis with the kids and silently led the march ML had planned. We were all so proud of her. There's no doubt in my mind that she secured a place of honor and respect worldwide that day.

She told the crowd, in part, "I come here today because I was impelled to come. During my husband's lifetime I have always been at his side when I felt he needed me, and needed me most. During the twelve years of our struggle for human rights and freedom for all people I have been in complete accord with what he stood for."

She went on to add, "Three of our four children are here today, and they came because they wanted to come. And I want you to know that in spite of the times he had to be away from his family, his children knew that Daddy loved them, and the time he spent with them was well spent. And I always said that it's not the quantity of the time that is important but the quality of time. . . .

"He was concerned about the least of these, the garbage collectors, the sanitation workers here in Memphis. He was concerned that you have a decent income and the protection that was due you. And this is why he came back to Memphis to give his aid."

And finally, she closed by saying, "He often said, unearned suffering is redemptive, and if you give your life to a cause in which you believe, and which is right and just—and it is—and your life comes to an end as a result of this, then your life could not have been lived in a more redemptive way. And I think that this is what my husband has done."

Later that day, rioting began in Memphis. Within two days, by April 6, riots had occurred in over one hundred U.S. cities, including Washington, D.C., Baltimore, Newark, Chicago, Kansas City, Boston, and Detroit. Dusk-to-dawn curfews were imposed across the nation, and President Johnson took to the airwaves to appeal for peace and calm.

On April 9, 1968 we laid ML to rest. The funeral consisted of two services; one at Ebenezer where the "Drum Major" tape was played, and the other on the campus of his beloved alma mater,

Morehouse College, where his mentor Dr. Benjamin E. Mays gave the eulogy. Mahalia Jackson rendered a solo.

Following the Ebenezer Service ML's body was laid on a mule-drawn carriage for the crosstown trek to Morehouse. The mule train was symbolic of his solidarity with the poor, "the least of these," the very people he had gone to Memphis to serve. It also was a reminder of the upcoming Poor People's Campaign which SCLC saw through after his death.

By now, everyone is familiar with the famous photograph of the hundreds of thousands of mourners who followed ML on his final March from Ebenezer to the Morehouse campus.

A FAMILY PORTRAIT TAKEN SHORTLY AFTER WE BURIED ML. AD, WHO WAS TO DIE UNBELIEVABLY FIFTEEN MONTHS LATER, IS TO CORETTA'S IMMEDIATE LEFT. ISAAC AND I ARE TO HIS LEFT. YO-LANDA, ISAAC JR, DEXTER, AND MARTIN III ARE IN THE SECOND ROW, LEFT TO RIGHT. BERNICE AND ANGELA ARE IN THE FRONT ROW, LEFT TO RIGHT.

After the service at Ebenezer, Mother and Daddy, Isaac and I, and a few other family members rode in a limousine to the Morehouse campus.

Because we traveled by limo and reached the campus well before the throng marching from Ebenezer, we were taken to the deserted Morehouse gym to await their arrival.

It was during this wait, and brief downtime, that the most humbling and poignant experience of my life occurred.

A nondescript, plain, simple lady appeared, no doubt there for the funeral. She saw us and, I'm sure, assumed that we had just arrived after marching from Ebenezer. She came in and said, "I know y'all must be tired. Please just let me rub your feet."

And she did. She bent over and tenderly, lovingly massaged my feet.

There was something almost biblical about it.

One of "the least of these," whom my brother loved so much that he was willing to die for them, had just unabashedly returned that love with the simplest, most profound gesture imaginable. I was speechless. I know that woman was an Angel, sent to comfort us in our hour of greatest grief and need.

The Lord does indeed work in strange and mysterious ways, his wonders to perform.

As we proceeded to Southview Cemetery, we were joined by Andy Young who was emotionally spent. I'm sure he hadn't slept more than a few hours in the past five days. What I remember most, is his dropping off to sleep during the ride to the cemetery.

The process of getting ML to his final resting place was emotional and complicated.

There is a back story to it. Shortly after ML was interred at Southview Cemetery, Reverend Fred Bennett, who had gone to

Memphis with us to retrieve his body, discoved bullet holes in the crypt during a visit to the gravesite.

Imagine that level of hate. What does it take to defile a grave and shoot into a crypt?

We decided we needed to move ML to a site adjacent to Ebenezer, where he would be more protected.

Again, consider the irony of that sentence . . . the need to be protected, even in death.

I assumed leadership, and coordinated this task. I orchestrated a series of early-morning quiet, dignified transfers of ML's body, under the cover of predawn darkness. I was joined in this labor of love by Coretta, my husband, Gladys Willingham—owner of Hanley's Funeral Home—several of her employees, and a few deacons from Ebenezer whom I had recruited.

We made these moves away from public view and outside of the prying eyes of the press. We wanted to afford the movement of ML's body the quiet dignity and respect he deserved.

We first moved him from Southview, temporarily, to a plot of vacant ground near Ebenezer.

A few months later, we moved him again. This time to a site a bit further up Auburn Avenue. This is the first site of which readers may have some recollection. It was at this location that we surrounded ML's grave with a simple white picket fence and an eternal flame.

During the construction of the King Center, and in preparation for placing ML's body in his final resting place, we moved him a third time. This time, he was still on Auburn Avenue, but we moved him a bit closer to Boulevard.

Finally, when the construction of the Martin Luther King, Jr., Center for Nonviolent Social Change was completed, we laid ML to

THIS PHOTO WAS TAKEN AT MY BROTHER'S TOMB.

rest at his present and permanent location: inside the crypt bearing the inscription "Free at last. Free at last. Thank God Almighty, I'm free at last."

He is now joined by Coretta and rests peacefully surrounded by the beautiful reflecting pool on the Center's plaza.

The fact that we were able to accomplish all of this with no publicity and without our privacy being invaded is a feat of which I am quite proud. ML was afforded the respect and dignity he deserved, and the King Center is now a marvelous testament to his life and work.

I take a great deal of satisfaction in how flawlessly we made all of this happen.

14

SO SOON AFTER LOSING ML:
MY BROTHER AD DIES

After ML's assassination, my family and I endured the sort of pain and massive void that only survivors left behind can truly know and comprehend. We tried our best to "keep on keeping on." There is no simple formula for grieving and recovery. So we each went through our own process of trying to heal. We leaned on one another and supported one another. We had always been a close-knit, warm, and loving family, but in those first few dark days, we found ourselves drawn even closer to one another for emotional support: Daddy, Mother, Coretta and her kids, Naomi and her children, Isaac, my children, and I all depended on one another and offered whatever support was necessary. We held our heads up and did, I suppose, as well as could be expected. We searched for a way to steady ourselves and learn how to keep moving forward.

Then, like a thief in the night, tragedy came to us and robbed us once more.

On July 21, 1969, while part of his family, together with Coretta and her children, vacationed in Nassau, AD was found dead, drowned in his home swimming pool.

He wasn't with the rest of the family because he'd departed early to return to Atlanta in order to participate in Ebenezer's Women's Day Program. He was now co-pastoring there with Dad. Little did any of us know, it would prove to be his final public appearance.

I got the news at Coretta's house, where I was then spending my days helping her organize ML's papers and beginning the work of creating the Martin Luther King, Jr., Center for Nonviolent Social Change. Coretta served as the founding president and CEO. Since its inception, I have served the center as treasurer. I was in the basement, and Angela and Isaac Jr., were with me when the terrible call came.

I remember repeating the same phrase over, and over, and over again. All I could utter was, "How can this be?" While I have no real memory of it, my son, Isaac Jr., says that I let out a disbelieving scream. He says, and I agree, it's the only time he's ever seen me react in such a manner.

AD was a good swimmer. This just made no sense at all. I simply could not grasp it. In some ways I still can't. I still have no explanation for how a competent swimmer just drowns alone in his own pool.

He was discovered by his son, Alfred III, who we all called Al. He had looked out the window early that morning and saw someone at the bottom of the pool. He rushed out, dove in, and identified his father.

Terrified, he ran back into the house and awoke his sister Alveda and his brother Derek, who now, coincidentally, serves as assistant to the pastor at Ebenezer Baptist Church, in Indianapolis, Indiana.

In yet another punch in the gut by cruel fate, it was Al's seventeenth birthday.

Alveda got on the phone and frantically started calling the family. As soon as I got the call I dropped everything. I left Coretta's, stopped to pick up Daddy, and continued immediately to AD's. We found Alveda, Al, and Derek in shock. Daddy did as fathers do. He tried his best to be strong for everyone. But all it took was a single look at his face to understand how much personal agony he was in. There was no way he could conceal the horror of losing another son. His only surviving son. The baby boy. And now—so very soon— after losing ML.

I tried to do all anyone can do in such a situation. I hugged and attempted to comfort the kids. I told them we'd get through it together and that we would be okay.

Alveda told us she'd been up late the night before talking and watching a television movie with her dad. She added that he seemed "unusually quiet," and that he wasn't particularly interested in what was on television. He wasn't his usual laughing, joking self. When she left him to go to bed he was sitting in an easy chair—just a routine Sunday evening at home.

Mother didn't come with Daddy and me. When they received the call at their house, before my arrival for Dad, it was clear something was horribly wrong. Mother just waited there alone, silent, for news from us at AD's. Now, on top of everything else, Daddy was going to have to break the news to her and tell her that their last son was now gone.

At AD's funeral, Daddy remarked how much he had lost, but

ANOTHER FAMILY PORTRAIT, THIS ONE TAKEN AFTER AD'S FUNERAL.

said that he was still thankful to God for what he had left. I can't begin to explain how difficult it is to cling to that outlook. But I've tried over the years to do just that. It has not been easy, and there were days when I came close to being overwhelmed, but I did what Daddy taught us, by word and by deed. I've remained thankful for what I have left.

DADDY WITH HIS "SONS," THE KING MEN, ML, ISAAC, AND AD. ALL GONE NOW, EXCEPT FOR ISAAC.

Unfortunately, we'd all be tested yet again as life continued. More tragic, unexplainable loss awaited us. So we set out trying to recover from the twin shocks of losing both ML and AD.

It sounds trite and simplistic, but I coped by taking whatever life offered—one day at a time.

And I would be remiss if I didn't stop here to offer another heartfelt, loving comment.

One of the things that has helped get me through this, and all the other challenges we've faced as a family, has been the steady love and support of Isaac, my husband.

Daddy said it better than I can. In his autobiography, *Daddy King*, he said:

> *I still had a son, of course, in Isaac, and he was an anchor for the family in these great storms not only for Christine, but for each of the rest of us. God had sent him all those years earlier, knowing we would need a man of character in times of hardship and sorrow.*

We did. And we would continue to need Isaac's loving presence and support, far too many times, in the not-too-distant future.

15

UNSPEAKABLE HORROR: MOTHER'S TRAGIC DEATH AT EBENEZER

The Chinese speak of the concept of yin and yang. The balance of life. The Bible says that "to everything there is a season." It's the idea that in this world, there is good and bad, joy and pain, evil and good. Like every human being, I have seen my share of the positive—and I've been confronted with negatives.

After ML was assassinated, and following our loss of AD, I thought the worst of it was behind me. I thought I had made it through the worst days of my life.

I was wrong.

Sunday, June 30, 1974, was without question the worst day of my life. There is no delicate way to phrase this, for that was the day my mother was murdered as she played the Lord's Prayer on Ebenezer's organ during the 11:00 A.M. worship service.

It was a normal Sunday, like any of the hundreds that preceded it.

My first inclination is to say I remember it like it was yesterday. But that wouldn't be entirely accurate, because there are parts of it

MOTHER DEAR: MY BELOVED
MOTHER, ALBERTA CHRISTINE
WILLIAMS KING. I MISS HER MORE
THAN MERE WORDS CAN EVER
FULLY CONVEY.

that are brilliant in their clarity, while other parts are draped in an overwhelming haze of darkness and disbelief.

Before we left for church that morning, we were rushing, like a majority of other American families, I'd venture to guess. We engaged in the universal routine of getting two children up and out for church. But this time there was a special bit of urgency, because Mother Dear, who had originally organized the ML King, Sr., Choir forty years earlier, would be accompanying them that morning as they sang. She was excited about reuniting with the choir, and we were excited about being able to be there and share in it.

Again, everything was totally routine and nondescript. I prepared breakfast for my brood, as always. It was likely bacon, eggs, grits, and toast. I'm sure I had coffee. I always do.

We loaded up in our green Ford LTD. It was a summer day in Atlanta, and naturally it was getting warm, even early in the morning. Kids being kids, Angela and Isaac Jr. complained they were hot. Isaac did what fathers across the world do—he told them if they were hot to roll their backseat windows down.

When we arrived, as was their routine, the kids went to the church nursery. Isaac Jr. found his cousin Dexter, I'm sure. Of course Mother and Dad were already there.

Normally, Daddy would have been in his customary place in the pulpit, leading the service as he had for years. That day, however, was different. He was scheduled to leave church early to get to the airport to catch a flight to New Jersey for an engagement. Reverend Dr. Calvin Morris, director of the King Center, filled in for him and was leading the service.

Accordingly, Daddy was seated in the front pew when we arrived. Mother was seated just feet away from the pulpit at the organ. Dad nodded and patted my leg twice as I joined him and took my seat.

In the next millisecond, my world changed forever.

The choir was just completing the Lord's Prayer, and a prayer was being offered. All heads were bowed and everybody's eyes were closed. At that instant a young, bespectacled black man who we now know to be Marcus Chenault, who'd been sitting in a pew close to the organ, suddenly leaped to his feet shouting, "I'm taking over here!"

My senses slowed to a crawl. All I could comprehend was that the tranquility of the Lord's house was being defiled by the obscene staccato sound of gunfire, *Pop! Pop!* . . . *Pop!* Over and over.

I can still hear the sound of his words and the gunfire.

Not once, but twice this madman screamed, "I'm taking over here!" Startled, we opened our eyes the second time he said it. At that point he was standing atop the pew where he'd just been seated. From his perch, he made his way to the pulpit and turned to face the choir.

I couldn't believe it. "Surreal" would be the understatement of the century.

This maniac was standing squarely in my father's pulpit. He

waved his weapon from side to side. Choir members ducked, ran, stumbled, crouched, and hid, anything to get out of the line of sight of this man waving a firearm. Then he shot the lady seated next to where he was standing, Mrs. Jimmie Mitchell. After that, he fired at Deacon Edward Boykin, before rushing into the pulpit. It seemed like I was watching a scene from a bad movie play out.

By now, his gun had been emptied of bullets. I didn't know it then, but two of his shots had found my mother. He had no more rounds left, and in a panic he rushed toward the exit behind the pulpit, which empties onto Jackson Street. Charging toward the exit, he knocked the Hammond organ over onto Mother. In the chaos, I didn't see it, but I learned later that Isaac had pulled it off her. As he was running down the steps to get out of the church he was finally caught and wrestled down.

I had seen Mother grab the right side of her face, though it didn't quite register at that instant. I didn't know what to make of it, or how to process it. It was difficult digesting everything that was unfolding around me. Whatever I thought, it was *never* that she would soon be lying lifeless at Grady Memorial Hospital.

I can't say who helped me up from my hiding place beneath the pew where I'd been pushed. Dazed, I was ushered out of the sanctuary and into the educational building. As my head began to clear I realized in horror that I didn't know where my children were.

"My children! . . . Where are my children?" I screamed. No one in the education building could answer my question; I tried making my way to the nearest exit. I was bumped, jostled, and pushed trying to get out of the building to look for the kids. I must have appeared as if I was losing my mind.

As I reached the doorway, someone brought Angela to me, and I was told that Isaac Jr. and Dexter had made their way to Daddy. "Thank God," I cried as I smothered her with hugs and kisses. There are no words to adequately convey how overjoyed I was that my children were unharmed and safe. I shudder to think what would have happened if they were not. My children are my world, and I can't allow myself to imagine what would have happened had they been hurt.

Angela was scared and upset. I tried calming her down, all the time not knowing what to do or say next.

Who can possibly know the "right" thing to do at a time like that?

I did my best. And that's all anyone could have asked.

While I was tending to Angela someone said I needed to get to the hospital. I didn't bother to question the advice; I just reacted and accepted it. Even in this mass confusion, I knew instinctively that all these stunned, frightened people had just gone through the same nightmare and were only concerned with helping. I have nothing but praise for all they did to assist me and my family.

What was replaying in my head were the screams, the sight of blood in the sanctuary, and the feeling this had to be fiction and not cold hard fact. It was totally unbelievable, and I kept asking myself, "Is this it—is the world somehow ending?"

I can't remember how, but I made it outside.

I couldn't believe my eyes. There were people everywhere. There was a throng of onlookers. When I looked in their eyes I saw what is often described as "the thousand-yard stare." It was a kind of blankness I had never seen before. They were bewildered and in shock. Many were crying; most had their hands pressed to their mouths in disbelief.

And the noise! There was cacophony and chaos. Screeching fire engines, wailing police sirens, the high-pitched blasts of police whistles, blaring automobile horns all combined to create a symphony of the sounds of turmoil.

I focused on the sight of Mother being placed in an ambulance. Daddy climbed in with her, as only one additional person was allowed to ride along.

One of our deacons, J. W. Mason, gave me a ride the few short blocks to the hospital. Isaac Jr. didn't ride with us. Somehow he and Dexter made their way there. Even today, I don't know how they managed to navigate through the mayhem to join us.

When we reached Grady I was ushered into a waiting room and was told Daddy was in the emergency room.

I tried to compose myself and sat there in the waiting room. Daddy sent word that he wanted me to come to him in the emergency room.

On the way, I heard an anguished cry. A woman's voice wailed, "Ed is gone! Ed's gone!" It was Mrs. Lois Boykin, a longtime Ebenezer member and the wife of Deacon Edward Boykin, who had been killed. I embraced and tried to console her.

I had no idea my own mother had not survived the rampage.

After spending a few moments with Mrs. Boykin, I went to the emergency room, where I found Dad sitting with ML's and AD's daughters, Yolanda and Alveda.

I asked, "Dad, how is she?"

"Christine, she's gone," he said.

It felt as if every bit of breath in my body had just been squeezed out of me.

Nothing, absolutely nothing, prepared me to *hear* those words, much less accept or believe them.

"She's across the hall. They'll let you see her," Dad said, still seated.

I left the room and stepped across the hall, still in a daze. Sure enough, there she was lying on a table. I embraced her still-warm body.

Eventually, Dad joined me and someone graciously escorted us to the chapel. A number of people were already there when we walked in. Most were from Ebenezer and many were crying. I have never been in a more bleak, depressing room in my life. We sang a hymn and offered a prayer.

How did a day that began with the promise of such joy end up with us all so pained in that room?

There never will be an adequate response to that question.

Marcus Chenault had been brought to the hospital and was being held in a room under police guard. Daddy wanted to see him.

This incredibly strong, brave, proud man wanted to see the assailant who had just taken his beloved wife of forty-eight years away from him.

And that's exactly what he did. In fact, he took Isaac Jr. and Dexter with him.

"Why did you do it? Please tell me, why did you do it?" To which Chenault replied, nonsensically, "I'm serving Jacob." And he repeated it. "I'm serving Jacob."

I am still at a loss to decipher the meaning of those words. I am no closer to understanding them now than I was thirty-four years ago when they were first uttered.

The remainder of that afternoon, the evening that followed, and the next day are among the longest, most dreadful hours of my life.

Deacon Mason, the same man who took me to the hospital, drove us to my parents' house when we left Grady. Still in utter shock and disbelief, I was stunned by the number of cars parked on both sides of the tree-lined street.

Mrs. Rosalynn Carter was among the first guests to arrive. Her husband, Governor Jimmy Carter, was out of town, and she conveyed their personal condolences. (Daddy and Jimmy Carter were friends, and three years later, Governor Carter would depend heavily on Dad as he undertook his successful presidential campaign. At the request of presidential nominee Carter, Daddy delivered the closing benediction at the 1976 Democratic National Convention in New York.)

A steady stream of guests, church members, and friends continued stopping by the house to pay their respects. Dr. Asa Yancey, Grady Memorial Hospital's medical director, brought Mother's jewelry and personal belongings. One thing he didn't have was the black dress with yellow flowers she had been wearing. It was being held as evidence by the Atlanta Police Department.

Before long, the Press arrived. Accompanied by Mayor Maynard Jackson, who stood by my side, I made a brief statement on behalf of the family.

Once I completed the Press statement, all sorts of jumbled thoughts cascaded through my mind. The reality of my mother's being gone hit me. What was I going to do without her; how was Daddy going to make it without his "Bunch" (Daddy's shorthand for "honey bunch")?

I had no answers to these questions, but the one thing I *knew* with all my heart was that I'd have to be strong. Obviously, Daddy needed me to be strong—I was the only child he had left. He's a rock of a man, but losing his wife and both sons put more on him than any one person should ever be called upon to bear.

I would have to guide and nurture my children through this, too, but clearly, Daddy and his well-being were my major concern.

I dug in my heels and got to work. I knew I'd have to do an emotional self-assessment. I was girding myself to get through the loss of my mother, as well as preparing to be a constant presence at Dad's side.

The following day, Monday, July 1, the *Atlanta Constitution* carried a lengthy front-page article whose headline screamed, "Gunman Kills Dr. King's Mother, Deacon During Church Services."

The story was unsettling to me for several reasons. First, in addition to recounting the horrid details of the shooting, it included a diagram depicting where the gunman had sat, just steps from Mother at the organ. That diagram really unnerved me.

Second, the article carried a chilling quotation from Chenault that demonstrated just how deranged he truly was. In reply to the question why he had shot my mother, he responded, "Because she was a Christian and all Christians are my enemies."

I must say this about Marcus Chenault. Over the years, I have been asked if I hate him. The answer is "no." More important, I have forgiven him. It's no easy task to get to the point of forgiveness. (I'll have more to say on the issue of forgiveness at a later point.)

With respect to hatred, I am of the firm conviction that there's just no place for it in the world. I have witnessed the devastating power of hate firsthand. Hate is inherently evil and destructive.

The only way we will ever be able to achieve peace is through love. It's so simple, yet so very difficult. We must learn how to love others as we love ourselves.

The pain of losing Mother wasn't over yet. We still had to say good-bye. We began that process at 7:00 P.M. on Tuesday, July 2, 1974, when we held her memorial service in Sisters Chapel on the campus of Spelman College.

The Reverend Joseph Lawrence Roberts, Jr., presided. The following year Reverend Roberts would succeed Daddy and become the fourth pastor of Ebenezer Baptist Church, but at the time, he was the staff director of the Presbyterian Church, U.S. Division of Corporate and Social Missions.

The organ prelude was performed by Dr. Joyce Finch Johnson, and Dr. Wendell P. Whalum, director of the famed Morehouse College Glee Club, directed their performance of the hymn "O God, Our Help in Ages Past."

Dr. Julius Scott, Jr., special assistant to the president of Spelman, led us in prayer.

Reverend Dr. Gardner Taylor read the Old Testament scripture, and the Reverend Dr. William V. Guy, pastor of Friendship Baptist Church and the father of actress Jasmine Guy, read from the New Testament.

We had an extraordinary rendition of "The Solid Rock." It was at once beautiful and heart-wrenching. The song moved me beyond belief, and each stanza evoked powerful memories of Mother and vivid pictures of treasured times. I was transported far beyond my seat in Sisters Chapel during those three or four minutes. It seemed as if my entire lifetime with Mother was encompassed in those few verses.

Mrs. Geraldine Moore performed a cello solo of "Jesus, Lover of My Soul." Her rendition was wonderful, heartfelt, and extremely touching.

Three distinguished gentlemen contributed reflections. They were Dr. J. Randolph Taylor, Pastor of Central Presbyterian Church and chair of the city of Atlanta's Community Relations Commission; the Honorable Walter E. Fauntroy, a former SCLC staff member and the District of Columbia's congressional delegate; and Spelman College president Dr. Albert E. Manley.

Finally, Dr. Benjamin Mays, president emeritus of Morehouse College, delivered the sermon. My family and I were grateful to Dr. Mays for the tremendous comfort we received from him personally, and from his words that evening. His sermon magnificently captured the essence of Mother. His words and his help were invaluable in assisting us through our darkest hours.

When we left the memorial service, we stopped at Ebenezer, where Mother had been brought to lie in state. We lingered for a few minutes to say our personal, private good-byes. Then we left for home to prepare for all that we would have to endure, yet again, in just a matter of hours. We still had the funeral to attend.

It was not an easy night for Dad or me.

The next morning we gathered at my parents' home for the funeral procession to Ebenezer. One of the first faces I recall seeing was that of the National Conference of Negro Women's Dr. Dorothy Height.

Reverend Andrew Young officiated. Andy, of course, is a trusted family friend who has been through so much with us. He was serving in Congress at the time and had not yet been appointed by Jimmy Carter as the U.S. ambassador to the United Nations.

Many dignitaries attended the services, including Mrs. Betty Ford, whose husband, Gerald R. Ford, was vice president of the United States. In just over a month, he would assume the presidency in the wake of the Watergate-related resignation of Richard Nixon.

The service opened with a prayer by Reverend Thomas B. Kilgore, chairman of the Morehouse Board of Trustees and pastor of the Second Baptist Church of Los Angeles.

The combined Ebenezer Choirs sang the beautiful hymn "Surely Goodness and Mercy Shall Follow Me."

I can hear the words now:

A pilgrim was I and a wandering; in the cold night of sin I did roam.
When Jesus the kind Shepherd found me, and now I am on my way
*   home.*
Surely, goodness and mercy shall follow me
All the days, all the days of my life.

By the time the choir completed their song I doubt there was a dry eye in the church. It was one of Mother's favorites, as were all of the songs on the program.

The Old and New Testament Scripture readings were by Mrs. Claire Collins Harvey, president of Church Women United, and Reverend D. E. King, pastor of Chicago's Monumental Baptist Church.

Mrs. Laura English Robinson added a note of comfort as she led the anthem "Lift Up Your Heads."

The first round of tributes were delivered by Mayor Maynard H. Jackson, Reverend Ralph David Abernathy, SCLC president and pastor of West Hunter Street Baptist Church in Atlanta; Reverend Dr. L. V. Booth, pastor of Zion Baptist Church in Cincinnati; and

Reverend Dr. John J. Mulroy, pastor of the Holy Family Church of Marietta, Georgia.

A song was then performed by the very choir Mother had been accompanying at the time tragedy struck. The Martin Luther King, Sr., Choir sang "He Will Remember Me." Jethro and Auretha English were the featured soloists. Mr. Arthur Neeley provided the accompaniment.

A second round of tributes were offered. They were given by Mrs. Laura Henderson, an Ebenezer trustee; Reverend Dr. Melvin H. Watson, pastor of Liberty Baptist Church in Atlanta, and Reverend Dr. Otis Moss, pastor of Second Mount Zion Baptist Church in Lockland, Ohio.

My father's dear friend Reverend Dr. Sandy F. Ray of Brooklyn's Cornerstone Baptist Church delivered the thoughtful, warm, and tender eulogy.

Following the eulogy, Daddy courageously made a statement on behalf of the family.

The recessional music was Dvorak's *Largo* from the *New World Symphony*.

Although the funeral had been necessitated by extraordinarily tragic circumstances, I was pleased with every aspect of the service. From the music, to the speakers, to the Scripture selections, I believe it accurately honored and paid tribute to Mother, and provided just the farewell we wanted her to have.

After the service, our family, various friends and guests, and the choir, still dressed in their black robes, made our way to Southview Cemetery, which is where a majority of our relatives are buried. Mother, likewise, is now interred there among its two hundred acres, just fifteen minutes or so south of Atlanta. Southview has a proud and unique history of its own, having been founded by former slaves. It was established shortly after Emancipation in 1886, with the idea that everyone, including the new freedmen, should be entitled to a dignified burial place.

Mother was placed in the same double mausoleum that just six years earlier had contained ML's remains.

Following the burial, we returned to Ebenezer for the repast. It had been a devastating, emotionally draining, very public few days. Now it was time to retreat into the comfort and security of family and familiar faces as we sought peace and an understanding of all we had just endured.

As you would imagine, the weeks that followed were difficult. But they were especially hard for Dad. One thing that is most prominent in my memory of that period, and for which I am forever grateful, is the care and support provided for us by aunt Woodie, Mrs. Woodie Brown of Detroit, Michigan. Aunt Woodie was Dad's older sister, who is now deceased.

Aunt Woodie came to Atlanta for the funeral and simply decided to put her life on hold and to stay with us to care for her brother. Her presence was comforting for us all, and it allowed me more time to spend with my immediate family, Isaac and the kids. She stayed almost an entire year. I will never forget her extraordinary act of kindness and selflessness in being with Dad. I am indebted to her, and her late husband, my uncle Jerome Brown. I can never thank them enough.

16

SUDDEN DEATHS OF A NIECE
AND A NEPHEW

On July 9, 1976, I was at Coretta's working. I was taking care of Coretta's books and financial matters, and working on matters related to the Martin Luther King, Jr., Center for Nonviolent Social Change. Angela was with me and just happened to telephone her younger cousin Jarrett, the son of AD's daughter Alveda King Beal.

When Jarrett answered, Angela could hear Alveda in the background screaming. It also sounded as if she was throwing something against the wall. When Angela asked what was going on, Jarrett told her it was because Alveda's sister Darlene, AD's younger daughter, was dead.

Darlene was a twenty-year-old sophomore at Spelman whose whole life was ahead of her. That afternoon she had gone to the athletic field at Southwest High School (since renamed Jean C. Young Middle School in honor of Andy Young's late wife). She was simply jogging around the track when she dropped dead of an apparent heart attack.

I told Angela to get her things. We had to leave immediately. We left Coretta's and rushed to AD's.

In 1986, exactly ten years after we lost Darlene, we were on the plaza at the King Center enjoying the Kingfest program one summer afternoon. Kingfest was an art and music festival coordinated by my niece Yolanda, ML's oldest daughter. Yolanda was an accomplished actress who had graduated from Smith College and was working as the King Center's artistic director.

We heard someone in the crowd saying that they'd heard on the radio that AD's son Al had died. The moment we heard it, I knew I had to get on the telephone to reach someone who could tell us that this awful news was just some kind of unfortunate rumor.

As I left the plaza heading for an indoor phone in the center, I met Andy Young coming down the steps to where we had been sitting. Looking forlorn and distressed, he was shaking his head. He told me it was true Al was dead. Angela and her cousin Bernice, ML's youngest daughter, let out anguished sobs when they heard the news.

In another cruel twist of fate, Al died exactly the same way his sister Darlene had passed a decade earlier. He was jogging around a well-known path at the Atlanta Water Works.

Same thing.

His heart just gave out. He collapsed and died instantly.

Al loved sports. I'll always remember, he was buried in a brown jogging suit and a basketball was placed in his hand, in the casket. His family knew he would have had it no other way. For those of us who knew and loved him, it was the perfect gesture.

17

LOSING DADDY

*W*hen the blare of the telephone awakens you in the middle of the night, it's rarely good news. I was in Oklahoma for a speaking engagement, and Angela was with me. We had finished dinner and were in bed back at the hotel.

Then the call came. I was told that Dad had suffered a "slight heart attack" and was at Hughes Spalding Hospital. It was after midnight and the airport was closed. I knew it would be morning before we could return to Atlanta. It's bad enough waking to that sort of news; the anguish is overwhelming, and its impact is multiplied exponentially when you're hundreds of miles and several time zones removed from your family. The feeling of utter helplessness covered me like a blanket. I knew I was in for a long, sleepless night.

Dad had reluctantly been trying to slow down. He had gone through previous problems with his heart and the doctors had assured us that they were minor. Everything was going to be fine—or so we were being told.

And now this—I couldn't believe it.

Fortunately, I was able to reach a nurse, who updated me on

Daddy's condition. Since I couldn't return home until the next morning, I had to cling to every shard of information I could glean.

In this case, "We've calmed him down and he's resting comfortably," was about all the nurse could tell me.

After a tense, sleepless night, we were able to leave on the morning's first flight back home. We left Oklahoma City's Will Rogers Airport streaking toward Atlanta.

The minute we landed, we went straight to the hospital. Dad remained there for a night or two before being released. Although he had stabilized, he still had a troubling heart condition. After he went home I watched him closely. Dad's house was only a half mile from mine, so I was constantly back and forth between the two.

For a while, he seemed to be getting along fine.

Then one night he called me and complained of chest pains. Isaac and I rushed over right away. I told him in no uncertain terms that we were going to the hospital. I called his doctor, who agreed with my decision.

We made a 911 call, and an ambulance arrived to transport us.

As the paramedics prepared him, they wanted to give Dad an injection. What followed was funny, humbling, and sad, all at once. When they tried to give him the shot, Dad grabbed Isaac's arm and said, "Don't let them stick me, Isaac, don't let them stick me."

Here was this mountain of a man, who had faced everything life had thrown at him, sounding like a little boy on his first trip to the doctor. Dad was afraid.

It took a while to find a suitable vein, and despite his protestations Daddy was eventually given the shot. He was taken to the hospital, admitted, and placed in intensive care. I stayed in the waiting area, tense, concerned, and on edge. By now it must have been three or four in the morning.

Suddenly, I was snapped to attention by the crackling of a PA alert: "Code Blue! Code Blue!"

I was approached by Daddy's doctor, Bernard Bridges, who told me Daddy had taken a turn for the worse. That scared me and put me even more on edge. I snapped into overdrive and went into emergency mode. I went to the phone and started alerting everyone I could think of. I called Coretta and Naomi. I called my children. I called Reverend Roberts. I called nieces and nephews. I called everybody!

Coretta was the first to arrive. Once everyone was there, we met in the waiting area and joined hands. Isaac suggested that we pray, and AD's son Derek led us. Just as we finished, Dr. Bridges came to us and told us Daddy had improved, taking a turn for the better. We all exhaled, sighed with relief, and thanked God. He told us we could see him, but only one at a time. We all spent some time visiting with him, and tried not to tire him out.

He remained hospitalized a day or so, recuperating from this scare. Then he was again released to return home. This time, once he got home, Derek and his wife were there staying with him fulltime. Of course, I'd go and check on him daily as well.

About that time, Isaac and I attended Morehouse's Homecoming football game to see Angela's majorette performance. We ran into a doctor friend, and I asked him what he thought about Dad's prospects, and what the best approach was at that point. The doctor advised us to watch him closely and to make sure he was as comfortable as possible.

The following weekend, I went by Dad's on Saturday afternoon and discovered that he had gotten much weaker. He said he wanted to take a bath and the caretaker wasn't there at the time. I'm not sure how I accomplished it, but I got him into the tub and managed to get the bed changed. I stayed until he went to sleep and then went back to my own home for the evening.

The next morning, I returned to Dad's and fixed breakfast. I took it to his bedroom so he could eat it there without having to move. I went back later and found that he hadn't eaten much, if any, of what I'd fixed. I encouraged him to try and eat something. He relented and took a small bit of orange juice.

He wanted to go to Salem Baptist Church, pastored by Reverend Jasper Williams. Salem isn't very far from the house, and when we arrived, there were a few deacons waiting outside to escort him in and make sure he was seated without difficulty. What I remember of the trip to Salem, again, is how weak he had become. He had difficulty getting down the steps and to the car. When we did finally reach the car, he slumped against it, totally winded.

I went back home and decided against going to Ebenezer, which was rare. I was exhausted from running back and forth between the two houses, trying to take care of my responsibilities at home as well as caring for my father. A few hours later I received a call from a young man who was an Ebenezer member and was with Dad. He told me Dad was back at home from church and added that Dad had a request.

Apparently, he wanted a strawberry milkshake and some fried chicken. I got dressed and went back over to Dad's. When I got there I found that he hadn't eaten much of the chicken, nor had he had much of the shake. He said he was tired and wanted to rest. I was again conscious of, and greatly concerned with, how weak he had become. I put him to bed and tried to clean up the house a bit. I washed the dishes and went into his bedroom to vacuum. It was at that point that I saw him gasping for breath.

Very worried, I asked, "Dad, what's the matter?" I gave him a sip of water and he confirmed, "I can't breathe."

Now I was truly terrified. I called out for Derek, who rushed into the room and said we needed to call an ambulance. He then started CPR. Dad didn't respond. Derek beat him in the chest, but to no avail.

An ambulance, followed by what has to be the longest fire engine I've ever seen, arrived. Angela, who was living on campus at Spelman, got there about that time. While they got Dad into the ambulance, Angela and I set out for Crawford Long Hospital and began the process of getting him checked in.

That's when I saw the ambulance pull up to the emergency room. The first thing I noticed was that there was no siren, no flashing lights. No sense of urgency. *Nothing.*

Instinctively, I knew something was wrong.

I completed the paperwork and a nurse took us upstairs so we "could be more comfortable."

We'd been there roughly thirty minutes when Dr. Bridges, accompanied by Dr. Calvin McLaurin, found me to say, "Christine, he's gone." Although, this time I wasn't shocked, I was deeply saddened. The death angel had visited again.

They dressed Daddy and told us we could go into the room with him. By now, all the grandchildren, Isaac, Naomi, and Andy Young were there. We called Coretta, who was in New York, and she told us she wasn't sure she could make it back that evening because all the flights had departed. She called back shortly afterward to tell us she'd, in fact, be able to make it after all. It turned out the airline was willing to hold the flight until she could get to the airport.

By the time we made it outside, the news media had gathered. I made a brief statement to the assembled Press. Hanley's Funeral Home, co-owned by a dear Ebenezer member, Ms. Gladys Willingham, came to retrieve the body.

That night, Sunday, November 11, 1984, we began the preparations for the funeral of Martin Luther King, Sr. I had to keep going.

We held the services at 11:00 A.M. on Thursday, November 15, at Ebenezer.

I rose early that morning. After I dressed, one of the first visitors to come by the house was Dr. George Napper, the Atlanta police chief. Dr. Napper was a former colleague on the faculty at Spelman. In addition to offering the standard condolences, he asked whether there was anything he could do.

THIS IS ONE OF MY FAVORITE PHOTOGRAPHS OF DAD, AND IT'S HOW I WILL ALWAYS REMEMBER THIS MOUNTAIN OF A MAN. HE SERVED AS SENIOR PASTOR OF EBENEZER FOR FORTY-TWO YEARS AND WAS MARRIED TO MY MOTHER FOR FORTY-EIGHT YEARS.

There was, and I'm grateful that he inquired. I wanted to see my father one last time. I knew, however, that this would be difficult and would present logistical challenges.

For a few precious minutes, I was alone with Daddy in our beloved Ebenezer. The privacy and the quiet time were priceless. I am forever indebted to Dr. Napper for making it possible.

After my interlude with Daddy, I exited Ebenezer and found myself in the midst of throngs of well-wishers who waved and held out their hands to me in a show of support. The love that poured forth from that crowd surrounding me was unbelievable. The feeling of comfort and warmth I received from them is simply indescribable.

Reverend Dr. Joseph Roberts, Ebenezer's pastor, officiated. The processional was "Variations on Amazing Grace." Reverend W. C. Smith, pastor of the Shiloh Baptist Church of Jonesboro, Georgia, offered a prayer. The choir sang one of Dad's favorite hymns, "I Will Trust in the Lord." They did a marvelous rendition. Daddy would have been pleased and proud. I certainly was.

Rabbi Alvin Sugarman from the temple in Atlanta read the Old Testament Scripture, from Isaiah 51:1–8:

> *Hearken to me, ye that follow after righteousness, ye that seek the LORD: look unto the rock whence ye are hewn, and to the hole of the pit whence ye are digged.*
>
> *Look unto Abraham your father, and unto Sarah that bare you: For I called him alone, blessed him, and increased him.*
>
> *For the LORD shall comfort Zion: he will comfort all her waste places; and he will make her wilderness like Eden, and her desert like the garden of the LORD; joy and gladness shall be found therein, thanksgiving, and the voice of melody.*
>
> *Hearken unto me, my people; and give ear unto me, O my nation: for a law shall proceed from me, and I will make my judgment to rest for a light of the people.*
>
> *My righteousness is near; my salvation is gone forth, and mine arms shall judge the people; the isles shall wait upon me, and on mine arm shall they trust.*
>
> *Lift up your eyes to the heavens, and look upon the earth beneath:*

for the heavens shall vanish away like smoke, and the earth shall wax old like a garment, and they that dwell therein shall die in like manner: but my salvation shall be forever, and my righteousness shall not be abolished.

Hearken unto me, ye that know righteousness, the people in whose heart is my law; fear ye not the reproach of men, neither be ye afraid of their revilings.

For the moth shall eat them up like a garment and the worm shall eat them like wool: but my righteousness shall be forever, and my salvation from generation to generation.

The Reverend Dr. E. R. Searcy, pastor of Mt. Zion Second Baptist Church in Atlanta, followed with the Scripture from the New Testament, II Timothy 4:1–8:

I charge thee therefore before God, and the Lord Jesus Christ, who shall judge the quick and the dead at his appearing and his kingdom;

Preach the word; be instant in season, out of season; reprove, rebuke, exhort with all long suffering and doctrine.

For the time will come when they will not endure sound doctrine; but after their own lusts shall they heap to themselves teachers, having itching ears;

And they shall turn away their ears from the truth, and shall be turned unto fables.

But watch thou in all things, endure afflictions, do the work of an evangelist, make full proof of thy ministry.

For I am now ready to be offered, and the time of my departure is at hand.

I have fought a good fight, I have finished my course, I have kept the faith:

Henceforth there is laid up for me a crown of righteousness, which the Lord, the righteous judge, shall give me at that day: and not to me only, but unto all them also that love his appearing.

In my opinion, nothing could have been more fitting, or more appropriate as a farewell and summary of Daddy's life and ministry. I obviously was not the only one in the sanctuary holding that thought, for, as Reverend Searcy, with his Bible tucked beneath his arm, turned to return to his seat, he was showered with "Amen," and "Well Done!" by the standing-room-only audience.

Next, the Martin Luther King Choir sang "I Love the Lord," which contained the words, "I love the Lord; He heard my cry and pitied every groan. And as long as I live, I'll hasten to his throne."

It was truly their finest hour, and the song was one of Daddy's favorites.

The first round of memorial tributes were offered by the following distinguished speakers: Mrs. Esther Smith, a member of Ebenezer and longtime family friend; Deacon Arthur Henderson; Mr. Jesse Hill, Jr., president of Atlanta Life Insurance Company and chairman of the King Center's board of directors; The Honorable George Herbert Walker Bush, vice president of the United States; Reverend Dr. Ralph David Abernathy, pastor of West Hunter Street Baptist Church and president emeritus of SCLC; The Honorable James Earl "Jimmy" Carter, Jr., former president of the United States; Reverend Dr. Melvin Watson, pastor of Liberty Baptist Church; and Reverend Dr. Marshall Lorenzo Shepherd, president of the Progressive National Baptist Convention, Inc.

Another emotional highlight followed when Ebenezer's favorite soloists, Auretha and Jethro English, mesmerized us all with the
beautiful "Old Ship of Zion."

After the stellar presentation by Mr. and Mrs. English, a second
round of tributes were offered by the honorable Joe Frank Harris,
governor of Georgia; Reverend Dr. Joseph L. Lowery, pastor of
Central United Methodist Church and president of SCLC; Reverend Dr. Charles G. Adams, pastor of Hartford Memorial Baptist
Church of Detroit, Michigan; the honorable Ivan Allen, Jr., a former
mayor of Atlanta; the honorable Andrew J. Young, the then-current
mayor of Atlanta; and Reverend Dr. Otis Moss, Jr., pastor of Olivet
Institutional Baptist Church in Cleveland, Ohio.

Mrs. Mary Gurley, a longtime member of Ebenezer and a con-
tralto in our choir, who also sang at ML's funeral, sang "God's
Amazing Grace." As always, she was magnificent. She has been a
family friend for as long as I can remember.

Dad's grandson, AD's son, Reverend Derek Barber King, delivered a heartfelt eulogy, the first of two. Derek, who was also executive director of Concerned Black Clergy, Christian Council of
Metropolitan Atlanta, did an excellent job and made us all proud.

The choir favored us with another most appropriate selection
for Dad, the spiritual "Ain't Got Time to Die."

Dr. Joseph Roberts followed with the second eulogy.

After all these poignant, beautiful tributes and eulogies, I had
the unenviable task of attempting to maintain my composure while
making a statement on behalf of the family. For people watching
on television and in the sanctuary, this was all part of the ceremony
in a well-choreographed service celebrating Daddy's life, but for me,
this was simply a daughter publicly taking part in the farewell rit-

ual for a father loved beyond compare and already terribly missed. I said, repeating one of Dad's favorite quotes, "Dad, we will keep the faith and keep looking up."

Reverend Dr. Albert Brinson, who was then pastor of the Bank Street Baptist Church in Norfolk, Virginia, led the benediction. As Daddy left Ebenezer for the final time, *Largo* from Dvorak's *New World Symphony,* ushered us out.

Throughout his long and fruitful life, Dad was active in a plethora of national, state, local, civic, and religious organizations. He was a life member of the National Association for the Advancement of Colored People (NAACP), a founder of the Progressive National Baptist Convention, Inc., and a member of the American Baptist Convention USA.

He served on the boards of directors of Economic Opportunity Atlanta (EOA), the Carrie Steele Pitts Home, and the Southern Christian Leadership Conference (SCLC). He was a member of the boards of trustees at Morehouse College and the Interdenominational Theological Center. He was an emeritus member of the boards of Citizens' Trust Bank and Atlanta University. He was honorary president of the Martin Luther King, Jr., Center for Nonviolent Social Change, Inc.

Dad received nearly a dozen honorary degrees and more than a hundred citations and awards. He was named the 1973 Clergyman of the Year by the Atlanta Council of Christians and Jews. In 1978, he was named Local and National Father of the Year in Religion by the National Father's Day Committee. In 1977, he delivered the sermon at Jimmy Carter's inaugural prayer service at the Lincoln Memorial.

Before I leave the topic, I must elaborate a bit more on the relationship between Daddy and Jimmy Carter. It was a warm, cordial one, based on mutual respect and common background. They were, after all, both country boys from small towns in Georgia—Daddy from Stockbridge and President Carter from the even smaller "metropolis" of Plains.

After the tremendous support and compassion he and his wife, Rosalyn, showed my family after the loss of my mother, the bond between these two men deepened and grew.

As Carter reached his decision to run for president, one of the first people he sought out was Dad. Governor Carter stopped in at Ebenezer one day and found Daddy in his study enjoying a quick catnap during the heat of a summer afternoon. They sat there, shooting the breeze, catching up on each other's lives, like any two friends who haven't seen each other for a stretch.

When the governor finally got around to revealing the reason for this visit and explained that he needed Daddy's support in his campaign for the presidency, Daddy was caught so totally off-guard that he replied innocently, "President of what?"

"The United States," Governor Carter replied, equally startled.

Dad told him quite candidly that he'd have no problem supporting him, so long as his tried and true friend, Nelson Rockefeller, the Republican governor of New York, didn't decide to seek the nomination of his party.

As word seeped out around the country that a former Georgia peanut farmer had the audacity to seek the highest office in the land, Daddy stood right there beside him, squarely in Jimmy Carter's corner. Daddy's confidence, support, and belief in Carter proved invaluable.

One specific instance when Governor Carter desperately needed

Daddy's assistance and endorsement occurred in April 1976 when, in response to a question about public housing, Carter stated that people should be "allowed to maintain the ethnic purity of their neighborhoods." Given the firestorm that erupted, you would have thought Carter had called for a national policy of apartheid.

Of course, he had done no such thing.

Carter knew it and Daddy knew it. On April 8, several days after the original comment, Governor Carter issued an apology. The apology did little to stem the tide of outrage or to calm the political opponents who sensed an opening to disrupt the campaign and bring Carter's bid for the White House crashing down in flames.

A rally in support of Governor Carter was hastily organized in Atlanta's Woodruff Park, which at the time was known as Central City Park. Dad was one of the featured participants at the rally. He made it a point to walk to the center of the platform and raise Carter's hand like a prizefighter's to declare, "The man has apologized. . . . He made a mistake. He's admitted he made a mistake. *We've got to forgive him.*"

I can't tell you the number of people who have stopped me in my travels around the country to tell me that Daddy's sincere statement that day made all the difference in their decision to cast their vote for Jimmy Carter for president.

Even with Daddy's unflinching support, Governor Carter still had to contend with a hostile perception of his candidacy, and with the fact that Georgia was steeped in a violent and racist past. He also had to confront the fact that the state regularly appeared last, or next to last, on evaluations of important social issues like education and health care.

Consequently, many people across the country were left with

nagging doubt and the question of how this peanut farmer from a backward place like Georgia could possibly expect to be the next president of the United States?

All I can say is *history speaks for itself.*

My next thought is to fast-forward to January 1977. The only words that come to mind are Cold . . . Cold . . . Cold! That was the weather that greeted us for the inauguration ceremony for Governor James Earl Carter as thirty-ninth president of the United States of America. I thought I was dressed appropriately for the occasion, and certainly for the weather. I wore a fur hat, I made sure my ears were covered, and I was wearing a fur coat that came to just below my ankles.

The problem was . . . *shoes.*

Mine were totally inappropriate—and strapless at that. To be blunt, I thought I was going to freeze, right there in the inaugural stands erected along the parade route on Pennsylvania Avenue.

Earlier that morning, Daddy had been the keynote speaker at a religious service held at the Lincoln Memorial. Leontyne Price performed a beautiful spiritual as part of the program. As I took in the sight of Daddy before the majestic Lincoln Memorial, I couldn't help but think back to ML, who fourteen year before had also given a speech of some importance in Washington.

Back to the funeral. Daddy was placed in the double mausoleum at Southview Cemetery next to Mother. Despite missing them both ferociously, I found the fact that they could be entombed there, side by side, for eternity extraordinarily gratifying.

After the burial, I experienced a few very rough hours. Isaac had to take his father and brother to the airport so they could return home to Missouri. For the first time since Daddy passed, I was totally, undeniably alone. It was only a couple of hours, but it seemed like a lifetime. It all came down on me at once—the grief, the pain, the silence, the void of his absence. Until then, there had always been someone around.

But not now.

The days immediately following Daddy's death were some of the most difficult days of my life.

It felt as if, without bothering to knock, grief had calmly decided to open my door, walked into my house, and stayed.

18

MY DEAR SISTER CORETTA

I liked Coretta from the start. I recall an early experience that won me over instantly. While visiting ML
in Boston, we went one day to pick her up for dinner. ML pulled
up outside and blew the car horn. Coretta took a good while to
come out and join us, and her point was made. She purposely kept
him waiting to emphasize that she expected him to come to the
door and "properly" call for her. I liked her approach to my brother.
My first impression was a good one. She was attractive and poised.
We had similar interests and our thinking was harmonious on a
number of topics. We hit it off instantly and bonded like old
friends.

I concluded not only that she was a wonderful young lady, but
also that my brother had done well. I was proud *of* him and happy
for him. I had never seen him so happy, nor as excited about any of
the women he had ever dated.

They were both young and in love. Bear in mind that ML was
the ripe old age of twenty-two; Coretta was just twenty-four.

Young or not, ML was the type who had to be certain before he made up his mind. In this case, it wasn't difficult. He was "definitely certain" about Coretta Scott of Alabama.

He was certain; she was "The One."

After they were married, and the kids came along, we started spending more time together because our children were all very close. They were more like siblings than cousins.

Due to her travel schedule, Coretta and I began our infamous telephone conversations. I became accustomed to receiving calls from her from all around the world *at all hours*—1:00 A.M., 3:00 A.M., 5:30 A.M., it didn't matter. Often, because of competing demands, it was impossible for us to be actually together face to face. For us, as the old advertising tag line went, long distance was indeed "the next best thing to being there."

Coretta was, in a very real way, the sister I never had. I could not have asked for a better, more dependable, more honest and supportive friend. I love her and miss her so very much. I am blessed to have known such a thoroughly beautiful lady.

While my brother made significant, world-changing contributions, Coretta did so, too.

I believe it is important that history accurately record her contributions and the extraordinary commitment, grace, and courage she always displayed.

Coretta and I shared so many special times together. We worked together in building the King Center. I was her personal bookkeeper and spent many afternoons in her home. We sat together in church. We talked a lot. We were real sisters. We literally traveled the world. For example, on November 30, 1982, we arrived in New Delhi, India. Our visit was brief but meaningful and memorable.

The trip was incredible. There we were in the land of Gandhi's birth. We had traveled to India for the world premiere of the film *Gandhi,* starring well-known British actor Ben Kingsley as Mohandas K. Gandhi, and our own Academy Award–winning Denzel Washington as ML. This was when I first met Denzel.

As soon as we arrived, we were taken to the residence of Prime Minister Indira Gandhi. This was my first time meeting Mrs. Gandhi, but Coretta had met her nearly twenty years before when she and ML were in India on a pilgrimage.

One of the movie's scenes depicted Gandhi making two-hundred-mile barefoot walk from village to village in 1947 for the purpose of personally convincing Hindus and Muslims to cease their senseless slaughter of one another. The scene was quite moving on an emotional level.

Both Mrs. Gandhi and President Zail Singh attended the premiere. The nonviolent theme of the movie was as relevant then as it had been in 1947 when Gandhi made the witness depicted. Little did we know that a scant two years later, on October 31, 1984, Mrs. Gandhi, the "Iron Lady of India," would be assassinated by two of her own bodyguards while walking the grounds of the very residence at which she had received us.

Our adventures around the world did not end there. Four years later, on September 13, 1986, Coretta and I found ourselves in Harare, Zimbabwe. We had been sent by the King Center, as part of an official delegation to South Africa, for the installation of Desmond Tutu as archbishop of Johannesburg. I was honored by being selected to be the formal head of our delegation. Traveling with us were members of the King Center board—Robert Brown, Carol Hoover, Dr. Bernard Lafayette, my nephew Martin III, our pastor, Dr. Joseph Roberts, and Barbara Skinner. Before reaching our final destination, we stopped in Zimbabwe. Our visit, coincidentally, co-incided with a summit meeting of the nonaligned nations.

The nonaligned nations, which by then numbered over one hundred countries, was an organization originally formed by such icons as Kwame Nkrumah of Ghana, Gamel Nasser of Egypt, and India's Jawaharlal Nehru.

Rajiv Gandhi, Mrs. Gandhi's son and himself then the prime minister, invited us to attend one of the sessions. Coretta decided to make a gift of some of ML's books to Mr. Gandhi and to present them at the meeting. That meeting turned out to be my first oppor-tunity to observe Cuba's Fidel Castro. We saw him along with the

THIS IS THE MOST OF THE KING CENTER DELEGATION THAT TRAV-ELED TO SOUTH AFRICA FOR THE INSTALLATION OF BISHOP DES-MOND TUTU AS ARCHBISHOP OF JOHANNESBURG. ALONG WITH MARTIN III, CORETTA, WINNIE MANDELA, AND I ARE BERNARD LAFAYETTE, BARBARA SKINNER WILLIAMS, REVEREND DR. JO-SEPH ROBERTS, AND BOB BROWN.

other leaders of the nations assembled there. Oddly, Castro maintained what could only be described as a grimace on his face. His expression didn't change the entire time we were in the room.

He just kept staring at Coretta and me as we moved about. It was strange, and the whole episode left me a tad unnerved.

A truly revealing moment occurred when Coretta expressed some concern about Rajiv Gandhi's having to carry the armload of books she had just given him. In a completely humble and unaffected manner, the prime minister replied. "I have two very good hands; I can carry the books myself. No problem!" It was a brief interlude before tragedy struck again. Six years later, in May 1991, Rajiv Gandhi would himself be tragically assassinated.

After our stopover in Zimbabwe, we spent several days in Johannesburg for the Tutu festivities. It was during this time that I met

HERE I'M SHOWN WITH CORETTA, MARTIN III, AND WINNIE MANDELA.

WITH WINNIE MANDELA, WHO EMBRACED ME, SAYING THAT, AS
ML'S SISTER, "YOU ARE THE BLOOD."

Winnie Mandela, as we traveled to Soweto while her husband, Nelson Mandela, the future president of South Africa, languished in prison on Robben Island. The authorities would not allow us to visit him there. Mrs. Mandela seemed particularly drawn to me. After she learned I was ML's sister, she enveloped me in a warm embrace, and said to me, "You are the blood."

She was a joy to be around. I am thankful I had the chance to get to know her. We were royally received in Johannesburg and Soweto, and both Mrs. Mandela and Bishop Tutu were appreciative of our presence.

Before returning to the States, we got to spend our final few days in Cape Town.

Cape Town is, by any measure, a simply beautiful locale. While we were there, a reception was held in our honor. It proved all the more special because it was on my birthday. To my immense surprise, a group of South African women at the reception presented me a birthday cake. I was stunned, and I wondered how they had any inkling of the significance of the day. It turned out that my ever-thoughtful sister-in-law, Coretta, had let them know it was my special day.

I should say a last word about our South African delegation, and that is to recognize the work of Dr. Ronald Quincy, who would later become the CEO of the King Center, in so expertly coordinating our travel.

My experiences with Coretta and world travel did not end there.

We once journeyed to Panama, at the invitation of Cirrolo McSwain, a former SCLC staff member. The trip was basically for relaxation, and it gave us the chance to see the Panama Canal. The highlight of the trip for me was a sumptuous dinner we shared one evening at which we were served the largest, most delicious lobster I've ever tasted.

Another time, after ML's death, I accompanied Coretta on a European concert tour, during which she was invited to speak at London's Saint Paul's Cathedral. We were joined by Coretta's sister, Edythe Scott Bagley. Also traveling with us were pianist/accompanist Russell Goode, Yolanda and her brother Martin III, King Center assistant Benita Bennett, and Joan Davies, who had served as ML's literary agent. The concert tour included not only the appearance in London but dates in Italy as well.

In August 2005, I was at home dressing to attend Spelman's opening day faculty luncheon when the telephone rang. It was Yolanda, who told me, "Mother is not talking, and I'm waiting for security to take her to Piedmont Hospital. I just wanted you to know." I told her at that the conclusion of the luncheon I'd call and check on Coretta. When I told Angela, who was at the luncheon, too, about Yolanda's call, she already knew of Coretta's condition. It seems that, somehow, Coretta's security had accidentally broadcast the fact they were taking her to the hospital on the wrong radio frequency. However it occurred, it was suddenly transmitted live across the airwaves.

When the luncheon ended, we went straight to the hospital. We found her pretty much unable to speak. She had suffered a stroke and remained hospitalized three weeks or more. I went to visit and check on her every day, without fail. I would complete my day at Spelman and then go to the hospital, where I would remain well into the evening. When she was released and allowed to go home, I continued to visit her daily at her condominium on Peachtree Street.

Coretta's children decided that it would be best to send her to Mexico for treatment. Angela, her daughter Farris (my granddaughter), and I went by to visit her the night before she left. She was in great pain and still not speaking. This would be the last time I saw her alive.

Shortly after Coretta was released from the hospital, a group of us set up a daily morning conference call where we would pray and check on her well-being. Among those participating were her sister Edythe; her brother Obie and his wife, Alberta Scott; Coretta's daughter Elder Bernice King; Yolanda; Carol Hoover; Patricia Lattimore, Coretta's personal assistant; and her private duty personal nurse.

On the Sunday before she died, we scheduled the call with

Coretta and Bernice in Mexico for the afternoon, rather than in the morning, so as not to interfere with anyone's church attendance. I will never forget that the nurse remarked on how well Coretta was doing. In fact, she was able to say a "good morning" to us, as I was in the car driving to Ebenezer and participating in the call. I spent my day feeling particularly upbeat and believing to my core that we were well on the road to improvement—if not recovery.

The next morning, we scheduled our call for eleven o'clock. I had a noon class that day and made sure I was settled in at the office in time for the call. The call was a few minutes late and it was getting near the time I had to begin my class. Coretta had not spoken yet, and I told the group I'd leave and get my class started, and then return to complete sharing in the conversation.

I did not hang up. I simply put the call on hold and did what I had to in order to get my class underway. By the time I returned, I was relieved to find Coretta on the phone.

She could speak, and was able to say, "Good Morning."

It was the final time I would hear her speak.

Finally, that night, as I was preparing for bed, I received a call from Delise Drayne, who works with my niece Bernice. She was calling from Mexico and said, "Bernice wanted me to call and let you know that Mrs. King has passed."

"What?" I said disbelievingly. "She died just a few minutes ago," was the response.

I screamed. Yet again, I had received a phone call bearing the news of the untimely loss of another loved one. I went into another room and gave the news to my husband, Isaac, who, as always, was there to provide a loving touch, a steadying hand, and the emotional support we all needed to get through this latest blow. Shock and numbness set in. Soon after I was notified about Coretta, Angela arrived at my house. She had received the news and knew I would need her support as well. Bernice had also notified Yolanda, Martin III, and Dexter.

The first thing we did was to get everyone on the phone. We started doing what we knew we had to do.

Bernice was the only family there with Coretta when she passed. We kept her on the phone until Yolanda and Dexter arrived.

Yolanda and Dexter were together in California, so they had the comfort of each other. They then set out, by car, for the facility in Mexico where Coretta had been receiving treatment. Incredibly, they stayed on their respective cellphones for the duration of their drive, and they joined right in with us in the planning for what we would do next.

We called Atlanta funeral director Willie Watkins, my former son-in-law, who had contacts with professional colleagues in San Diego who could help us retrieve Coretta's remains to be returned to the United States.

Bernice learned that she couldn't be released immediately. Mexican authorities required an autopsy first. That meant Coretta's return was delayed a day so the autopsy could be completed. The minutes of the wait seemed like days—if not *months*. I don't have the words to express how frustrating it was, waiting through the delay in Coretta's being returned to us. I ultimately did not need to resort to it, but I'll admit I considered contacting the White House to ask for high-level intervention in assisting us in expediting Coretta's return. Finally, somehow, special permission was granted for her release.

During that long night on which she passed, and on that hours-long telephone call, we put together the press release announcing Coretta's death. It was an all-night affair.

Bernice, Dexter, Yolanda, Martin III, and Bishop Eddie Long were finally able to get Coretta back to Atlanta. They traveled on Bishop Long's private plane, and Coretta flew separately on a cargo jet, which made it possible for us to bypass the horde of reporters and press covering the event.

That moment, too, was full of sadness. The flight from Mexico arrived at Atlanta's Fulton County Airport at about 3:00 A.M. For the most part, I was doing okay, until I approached the airport. It was at that point that I was overwhelmed.

The finality of it all hit me—I was there to greet my sister's body. I was reduced to uncontrollable tears. I had to remain in the car for a few minutes, alone and lost in my tears and grief.

I knew I couldn't meet the plane like that. I had to compose myself and be strong for the kids. Finally, the plane with her body arrived. It seemed so huge, and the casket with her body seemed so small. Again, I was simply overwhelmed.

The plane was taken to a hangar for unloading. To this day, I am convinced that it was the biggest, tallest airplane ever constructed. I had to strain my neck to peer upward watching Coretta's casket being unloaded. Again, I was struck by how incredibly large the plane and the machinery to unload it seemed.

By comparison, her casket, and those of us there to greet her, seemed so very, very small.

It was just all too much.

When we left the airport, we were able to spend a few final, quiet moments with Coretta, at the Watkins Funeral Home. It made all the difference in the world for us.

We remain forever grateful for those few precious, quiet moments.

Later that day, we shifted into overdrive in order to plan the funeral.

As the world saw, it was held at Bishop Long's New Birth Missionary Baptist Church. It was attended by, among others, President and Mrs. Jimmy Carter; President and Mrs. Bill Clinton; President and Mrs. George W. Bush; President and Mrs. George H. W. Bush; Stevie Wonder; and a host of other celebrities, civil rights movement icons, and thousands of ordinary citizens who just wanted to express their love and appreciation for Coretta and her life's work. Among the notable guests who joined us in saying good-bye were Maya Angelou; Yolanda's former theatrical partner, Attallah Shabazz, daughter of Malcolm X and Dr. Betty Shabazz; and Dr. Dorothy Height, all of whom spoke.

Bernice gave a loving warm, reflective, and thought-provoking eulogy for her mother. I was among those who gave tributes.

I miss my sister dearly.

I am eternally thankful that she came into our lives and for the times we shared, the good times and, yes, even the bad. From the beginning, she was a gift, a blessing, and a treasure. She enriched our lives tremendously. She brought joy, inspiration, and pride.

Not long after the funeral, we were able to stay true to Coretta by fulfilling her last great wish. From the conception of the King Center, she always knew that when her time came she wanted to join ML and be buried at his side.

It only makes sense—there are some relationships bound to exist for eternity. And so it is with ML and Coretta. They now rest together, side by side, in a double mausoleum on the grounds of the center.

And that's as it should be.

Getting Coretta to her final resting place was not a simple undertaking. Yolanda courageously took the lead in coordinating the many entities that had to be involved to make the transfer the dignified effort Coretta deserved. We were assisted immensely by National Park Service superintendent Judy Forte, the African American woman in charge of the King Center Historic District. We moved Coretta late one evening. A small group of family was on hand to observe. It included my granddaughter Farris, my children, Angela and Isaac, Jr., Yolanda, Bernice, and me. It goes without saying it was a very emotional evening for us all.

We all miss her so very much. It's no cliché; she is truly irreplaceable and was one of a kind. We won't see the likes of her again.

ANOTHER DEATH FROM OUT OF THE BLUE:
YOLANDA DENISE KING

*I*t started with the telephone again. It was May 15, 2007. By now, I really should have developed immunity to, if not a phobia about, a phone ringing unexpectedly. God knows I've had enough experience with these calls. This time it was ML's youngest son, Dexter, calling from California with the news of fate's most recent incomprehensible body blow. I had just come in from an evening revival at Ebenezer.

"Aunt Chris, Yolanda has fallen. She's not breathing," he said. "I can't get her to breathe," he repeated, "I can't get her to breathe."

Dexter told me he'd already tried to reach his brother Martin III and Bernice, his younger sister. Then he'd placed a 911 call and phoned me. As we were talking, the ambulance arrived and he told me he'd call me back.

Once they reached the hospital, Dexter did indeed call back. By this time we arranged a conference call. Bernice and Martin III had been notified. Most of the family was on the call: me, Bernice, Martin III, Angela, Isaac Jr., and Alveda.

Dexter told us they had taken Yolanda to the emergency room, and that once more, he'd call us back when he knew more.

We all waited with bated breath and with our stomachs twisted in knots. We couldn't believe it.

When Dexter's call finally came, he said simply, "I'm going to put the doctor on and let him speak to you all."

I was not in the least prepared for the bomb that would be dropped with the next words.

The doctor explained that they had done everything they possibly could, that they had tried everything, but that she simply didn't respond. They could not revive her.

The doctor told us, "I'm sorry, she's gone."

ML and Coretta's firstborn, Yolanda Denise King, was dead.

She led an extraordinarily rich and textured life that mirrored the very evolution of the modern civil rights movement. She entered the world on November 17, 1955, a scant two weeks before Rosa Parks set in motion the events that would thrust Montgomery, the bus boycott, and ML onto the world's stage. Given Yoki's career choice, and her own very specific, very unique contributions to the movement, I cannot use a more appropriate and fitting word than "stage" to begin attempting to place her life into proper perspective.

When she was barely two months old, as I recounted previously, ML and Coretta's home was bombed. We've always known that it was by the grace of God that this precious child wasn't harmed by that cowardly act.

By 1960, ML and Coretta relocated to Atlanta, where Yolanda became involved in various activities at Ebenezer. She attended Sunday school and was active in the youth group and the Youth Concord Choir.

I remember when Yoki became enamored of a local amusement park called Funtown, which had recently opened. Like all kids, she wanted to experience the midway, the cotton candy, and the bumper cars. That left to her parents the difficult task of explaining that she could not be admitted to the park like other children, because of the color of her skin.

As upset as his child, ML cited this experience in his "Letter from a Birmingham Jail." He attempted to explain the urgency of confronting segregation and discrimination by recalling this humiliating dilemma, writing:

> When you suddenly find your tongue twisted and your speech stammering as you seek to explain to your six-year-old daughter why she can't go to the public amusement park that has just been advertised on television, and see tears welling up in her eyes when she is told that Funtown is closed to colored children, and see ominous clouds of inferiority beginning to form in her little mental sky, and see her beginning to distort her personality by developing an unconscious bitterness toward white people . . . then you will understand why we find it difficult to wait.

In early 1963, Funtown quietly desegregated. Yolanda and her siblings, Martin III and Dexter, got to make the trip when ML and Coretta were at last able to take them for a day of pure enjoyment. The children had a wonderful time.

And so did their father.

Early on, Yolanda began delighting her family by writing and directing plays in which she cast her often reluctant brothers, sister, and cousins. At eight years old, she was enrolled in Atlanta's only integrated drama school, the Actors and Drama Workshop. The enterprise was run by Walter and Betty Roberts, parents of well-known actors Eric and Julia Roberts. That same year, she wrote her first play. It was about a queen who learned about diverse cultures by receiving visitors from other countries. Her siblings were supporting cast members, but the role of the queen was strictly reserved for Yolanda.

I can't say all her productions went off without a hitch. At eleven, her backyard version of *Sleeping Beauty* ended abruptly, when the script required six-and-a-half-year-old Dexter to awaken his sister, Bernice, aka Sleeping Beauty, with a kiss on the lips.

Dexter without hesitation threw his script on the ground and ran into the house. I imagine the director was pretty much left shouting, "Cut!"

I also remember when Yoki first learned to play the piano. She couldn't wait to display her newfound musical talent. The same was true with her early exposure to dance. She was so excited to show me her elegant little pirouettes. Even then, she was the featured performer in her one-girl shows.

Yolanda attended Atlanta's Grady High School where she made a lifelong group of friends who came to be known as the "Grady Girls," including one local television newscaster, Angela Robinson, who later presided at her memorial service.

Yoki threw herself into extracurricular activities in high school with a passion. She was on the student council and served as co-president of her senior class. During her senior year, at just sixteen, and defying all odds, she made her dramatic public debut, performing in a production of *The Owl and the Pussycat*. She was cast as a prostitute and her character was required to kiss a white boy. The scene, like the play itself, caused an awful uproar in the community. But, it was Coretta who taught her the lesson of being true to herself, by encouraging her to follow her own dreams despite naysayers, and to not allow herself to be defined by the limited perspective of others.

Yolanda graduated from Grady in 1972.

After leaving Grady, she went off to the all-female Smith College in North Hampton, Massachusetts. She graduated from Smith in 1976 with a B.A. (With Honors) in Theater and African American Studies.

Then, following her dream, Yoki moved to New York, where she attended New York University. She graduated in 1979 with a Master's in Fine Arts. While in New York, she met and became dear friends with Attallah Shabazz, one of the six daughters of Malcolm X and Dr. Betty Shabazz. Yolanda and Attallah cofounded the Nucleus Theater Group.

Yoki left New York and returned to Atlanta, where she became the first director of cultural affairs for the King Center. In a sterling demonstration of her commitment and dedication to the cause of art in furtherance of the quest for justice, she remained in this capacity, working pro bono, for almost ten years. Yolanda was dedicated to using her art for the promotion of social change. Under her leadership, a number of innovative programs were implemented. I mentioned Kingfest earlier and there was also a companion Kingfest, International.

She also started a Nonviolent Film Festival and the "Dream Team." The Dream Team consisted of professional actors who produced and performed humorous vignettes about social issues. Her goal was to bring people together through the arts and to celebrate the diversity and commonality of all humankind.

Yolanda left the King Center in 1990, and for three years was professor in residence in Fordham University's Drama Department. While at Fordham, she produced and directed several plays, including *A Raisin in the Sun* and *Angels in America*.

When she left Fordham, she moved to Los Angeles, where she founded Higher Ground Productions to "educate, empower, and entertain," as she so often said. Yolanda's innovative lecture-performances, which she termed "edutainment," were applauded throughout the United States as well as in venues in Europe, Africa, and Asia.

In 1991, at the National Black Theater Festival in Winston-Salem, North Carolina, she premiered *Track: A Celebration of the Triumph and Spirit of Martin Luther King, Jr.* It was a one-woman multimedia show, in which she played sixteen characters. For four years after that, Yolanda toured the country with *Track,* and performed at such historic locales as the Kennedy Center in Washington, D.C., and Lincoln Center in New York City.

During the 1996 Olympics, Yolanda premiered one of her most memorable theatrical productions, *Achieving the Dream,* which she cowrote with Cheryl Adam Odeleye. In the play, she portrayed several characters from the civil rights movement, including a girl who rides a desegregated bus for the first time and an activist who reacts to the racially motivated bombing of the Sixteenth Street Baptist Church in Birmingham.

The body of her work—Yolanda's stage, television, and film credits—reflects her commitment to social change. There were, for example, her portrayals of Rosa Parks in the NBC-TV movie *King* and of Dr. Betty Shabazz in the film *Death of a Prophet* with Morgan Freeman, and her appearance with Medgar Evers's daughter, Reena, in *Ghosts of Mississippi,* directed by Rob Reiner.

On the CBS television series *JAG,* she played Judge Esther Green. She also played the title character in the short feature film *Odessa.*

In 2003, she published her first book, *Open My Eyes, Open My Soul,* coauthored with Elodia Tate. In 2005, she published a second book, *Embracing Your Power in 30 Days,* coauthored with Wanda Marie.

In 2006, Yolanda's company, Higher Ground Productions, co-produced, with Agape International Spiritual Center and Vema Jones, *A Call to Consciousness,* a day-long series of workshops and performances celebrating the twentieth anniversary of ML's birthday as a national holiday.

Yolanda Denise King was a member of the board of directors of the King Center. She served on the Partnership Council of Habitat for Humanity, was a member of the Southern Christian Leadership Conference, and was a sponsor of the Women's International League for Peace and Freedom. She held a lifetime membership in the National Association for the Advancement of Colored People.

And beyond all those formal qualities, she was a beautiful spirit, a joy to be around, who was capable of brightening up even the darkest circumstance. We were all blessed to have known and loved her, and no words can ever convey the void in our lives since she left us.

I loved her, miss her, and think fondly of her magnetic presence every day of my life.

WORKING THROUGH PAIN
AND GRIEF AND THE JOURNEY
TO FORGIVENESS

At some point, the realization of it all hit me. The void left by the absence of so many loved ones was like ice-cold water washing over me, cascading like a turbulent untamed tidal wave. Daddy was gone. Before him, it had been Mother Dear. Before her, there was AD. Before AD, there had been ML; along the way, there were Darlene, Al, Yolanda, and Coretta. How could this be?

How could one person be expected to withstand such pain and loss? My world had been turned upside down, over and over again. There were times I felt as if I were paralyzed. There were certainly times when facing another day seemed virtually impossible. Some days, I found myself unwilling to even conceive of, or think of, facing tomorrow.

Somewhere during the course of this struggle, I knew I'd have to pull myself together. I had to regain my emotional balance. I had to compose myself and keep moving forward. I could not allow myself to be lost. I could not afford to be no good to myself, no good for Isaac, and no good for my children.

I knew I had no choice but to come back to myself—for them.

By the grace of God, I did make it, over and over again. I made it. And, I am continuing to march forward every day. In every possible way.

One of the fundamental building blocks to just maintaining myself was taking to heart Daddy's admonition not to hate. "Don't *ever* hate," he said so often. And he never wavered. On this point he was crystal-clear. This from a man who had himself lost so very, very much. He had buried both his sons and his wife of forty-eight years. He was once asked if he hated James Earl Ray, the convicted murderer of ML, and Marcus Chenault, the assassin of my mother. His answer was, "I don't hate either one. There is no time for that, and no reason either. Nothing a man does takes him lower than when he allows himself to hate someone."

In his book, Dad said, "If we achieved a victory in the South it was over inhumanity. When the evil heart of segregation could beat no more, it was because it had been stopped by people who did not counsel violence, who did not brutalize and bomb, who never sought to take away any part of anyone else's identity as a human being. These things triumphed over the exaggerated power of hatred. And so, which path would any man who knew this choose to travel? Hatred did not win. I prefer to share the triumph."

My father was a wise and profound man. I knew that I wanted to share in this triumph. I knew I had to move on.

This idea of forgiveness can be a tricky thing. It is always challenging and often difficult. But if it was easy, it wouldn't be called struggle, would it?

The road to forgiveness is not easily traveled. I discovered that there are times in life when forgiveness is both vital and absolutely necessary. Otherwise, you find yourself confined to darkness.

Ultimately, I did emerge from the shadows, and back into the light.

On the pages that follow, I discuss what I've done with the rest of my life.

There's the story of the birth and development of the Martin Luther King, Jr., Center for Nonviolent Social Change; there's the joy I found in seeing the Martin Luther King, Jr., Child Development Center take life; there is my looking back across the panorama of my life as the sole survivor of my siblings, and my role as the matriarch of my family; there is the pride in seeing my children and my nieces and nephews successfully reach adulthood and pursue callings and careers of their own.

There is the satisfaction and triumph in knowing that I am, indeed . . . *Still Standing Through It All.*

20

WORK AT THE MARTIN LUTHER KING, JR., CENTER FOR NONVIOLENT SOCIAL CHANGE

*A*fter ML's death, we knew we'd have to find a way to institutionalize his work and to preserve and carry on his legacy. Coretta accomplished this Herculean task by conceiving and creating the Martin Luther King, Jr., Center for Nonviolent Social Change. The center is located, quite appropriately, at 449 Auburn Avenue, in Atlanta, just a few blocks from the home in which we were all born, and on the same block as Ebenezer Baptist Church.

The center's beginnings were humble and were achieved by taking small steps. Not long after we lost ML, Coretta threw herself into action. She called together a group of trusted friends and advisors to discuss how we'd go forward with protecting his legacy and completing the unfinished work. Among those taking part in our initial conversations were Dad, Dr. Benjamin E. Mays, President Albert Manley of Spelman College, Andy Young, and Jesse Hill.

In reality, the King Center was born in the basement of Coretta's house. In addition to not having a better option at the time, as a practical matter, it made immense sense. Quite frankly, that's where everything was located. There were boxes upon boxes, papers, speeches, notes, correspondence, clippings, files, and other types of records. *Everything.*

In fact, that basement was in the news not so long ago. That very location held the bulk of the material that has come to be known as the Martin Luther King Papers. These materials were recently purchased by the city of Atlanta and made a part of the Martin Luther King, Jr., Collection at Morehouse College.

Because of my background in economics and finance, I have been intimately involved with the center since it was conceived. I have served as the only treasurer the institution has known.

As I mentioned in a previous chapter, I started out doing all of the bookkeeping from Coretta's basement. That is why I was there when we got the news about Darlene's death. Primarily, on a daily basis, I would go to Coretta's after putting in a full day teaching my classes at Spelman, gathering up my children at Oglethorpe Elementary School and bringing them along with me. I often worked late into the night, not departing for home until the wee hours of the morning.

Long after outgrowing the stifling confines of the basement, we moved to the lower level of the Gammon Theological Seminary, part of Atlanta University's Interdenominational Theological Center (ITC).

As we outgrew ITC, we relocated to a house next door to our birth home on Auburn Avenue. This space was more conducive to our work. It was fairly large; I had an office, and Coretta had one, too. It had a conference room, and there were a number of smaller offices as well. We used the conference room frequently for meetings with the architect and with the builder as we prepared to construct the center on its present site.

As treasurer, I was responsible for handling, accounting for, and dispersing all the funds that were used for the center's development and construction. Everything had to be painstakingly accounted for; the sheer volume of the required accounting was massive.

I will never forget my dealings with the Trust Company Bank. Due to the large quantity of public funds involved in the center's construction, the Trust Company performed an oversight role.

Let's be blunt here. These were exclusively white males in business suits, who never resisted attempting to employ intimidating tactics. I used the phrase "attempting" purposely, because they didn't work. When I walked into our meetings, as the lone black woman present, all eyes were on me. I had no fear whatsoever.

During one such meeting, one of the bank's representatives brusquely proclaimed, "You'll have to let some staff go."

At issue were some funds that had not arrived—and possibly would not come at all.

I calmly informed that gentleman, "We can't do that. We'll just have to find another way!"

And we did.

There came a point when Dad could see how overwhelming my cycle from home, to Spelman, to the center, to Coretta's home and back again had become. He suggested I lessen my workload at the center to allow for more time with my family. I considered it, but really did not feel I could do it at the time. So I passed on the idea.

We had to make occasional reports to the Better Business Bureau. I was the one who represented the center in making these reports. I'm proud of the fact that we consistently received high ratings. The board of the King Center was so pleased with my work that they suggested that I give up teaching at Spelman in order to work full-time at the center. This was no subterfuge or effort to steal me away from my career. Dr. Donald Stewart, who was Spelman's president, was also a board member of the King Center.

Later the same week, Dr. Stewart called me into his office to say he didn't think "I wanted to give up my career as a teacher." I assured him empathetically that I did not. He asked how he could help to ease my burden and workload at the center. I told him what I needed was a good financial person. Dr. Stewart took me to chief financial officer Robert (Danny) Flannigan's office at Spelman and asked whether Danny knew anyone who could perform the financial role. Danny did, and recommended a gentleman named Isaac Clark at ITC. Mr. Clark was interested in the position. We quickly interviewed him and in no time, he came aboard.

In addition to my financial obligations at the center, I was also involved in developing some of the programmatic aspects. I helped to develop our workshops on nonviolence, which took place during the summer. We taught the six principles of nonviolence to students of all ages—youths and adults. We also taught aspects of conflict resolution in these workshops.

Our first nonviolent workshop was challenging and exciting. We were breaking new ground in terms of curriculum. It also resulted in one of the funniest one-liners I have ever heard.

We invited the heroine of the Mississippi Freedom Democratic Party, Mrs. Fannie Lou Hamer, to attend. Mrs. Hamer had burst into the national consciousness at the 1964 Democratic National Convention when she led the challenge to the seating of Mississippi's all-white, segregated, exclusionary convention delegation. She

ME WITH MRS. FANNIE LOU HAMER, ACCOMPANIED BY HER GRAND-
DAUGHTERS, ATTENDING OUR FIRST SUMMER WORKSHOP ON NON-
VIOLENCE SPONSORED BY THE KING CENTER.

became a national treasure when, in testifying before the DNC's
Credentials Committee, she proclaimed, in an immortal phrase,
"I'm sick and tired of being sick and tired."

Mrs. Hamer brought her grandchildren with her to Atlanta to
the workshop. She was a modest, humble person, and a joy to be
around. One day, during the workshop, we had the opportunity to
introduce Mrs. Hamer to Mother.

I'll never forget the moment they met. Mrs. Hamer said innocently, "You're Martin Luther King's mother ... and you're not
even stuck up."

I loved it!

Incidentally, I was the first recipient of the Fannie Lou Hamer
Award at Spelman College. This award is presented annually to a

member of the Spelman community in recognition of community service contributions outside the Spelman community.

Before I leave the subject of the King Center and its creation, along with the evolution of the entire surrounding area, I must give another bit of credit where it is due.

Much credit is due President Jimmy Carter, for it was he, unbeknownst to most, who came up with the idea of establishing the Martin Luther King, Jr., National Historic Site. The idea of such a thing had never occurred to Coretta or my father, and certainly not to me.

The president thought it would be a good idea and urged us to at least look into it. And as we do with all things in our family, we thoroughly considered the pros and cons of the idea. We ultimately agreed to do as President Carter suggested and looked into the idea with an open mind. President Carter took care of all the arrangements.

At his suggestion, Coretta and I visited two national historic sites.

Our first stop was Springfield, Illinois, and the famous log cabin—Abraham Lincoln's birth home. We found the cabin quite well organized. Each of the rooms was named. We found one of particular interest—the "Girl's Room." According to our tour guide, as well as the accompanying signs, this room was home to a teenaged "immigrant girl," who would stay overnight and help with various household chores: She did cooking, scrubbed floors, and washed clothes by hand, using the backbreaking washboard. The tour guide added the detail that these difficult chores often left the poor girl's hands and feet swollen. I thought it contributed a humanizing touch, and obviously, I still recall it these many years later.

WITH PRESIDENT CARTER, WHO SUGGESTED THE IDEA OF THE
MARTIN LUTHER KING, JR., NATIONAL HISTORIC SITE.

We spent the bulk of that day touring and asking lots of questions. Coretta remarked, privately, that nowhere in the literature on the girl's room was the young teen ever characterized as a "slave girl."

Overall, we found our tour of the Lincoln site quite enjoyable. Naturally, the historical parallels between ML and President Lincoln were fascinating.

After finishing our day in Springfield, we flew to Washington. We again visited our national memorial sites and monuments, including the Lincoln Memorial, Jefferson Memorial, and the Washington Monument.

We stayed overnight in Washington and then set out the next morning for Texas. This time, our destination was the Lyndon Baines Johnson National Historic Site in Austin.

Our first stop was the Johnson Presidential Library, at which the brilliant and outspoken former congresswoman from Texas, Representative Barbara Jordan, warmly greeted us. Congresswoman Jordan was at the time serving as the presidential scholar-in-residence at the library. Coretta and I were excited to spend some time with her, and I'm sure the feeling was mutual. She gave us a personal tour of the library and we peppered her with questions about it: its setup, scope, and operation. We had a wonderful day exploring and reminiscing. We had all seen and experienced so much in our lives. We agreed that there are times when survival can be painful, to be sure—but it is also extraordinary and wonderful.

After our day at the library, we went to the LBJ Ranch, where we

CORETTA AND I ARE SHOWN WITH AN ARCHITECT'S RENDERING OF THE MARTIN LUTHER KING, JR., CENTER FOR NONVIOLENT SOCIAL CHANGE, ATLANTA, GEORGIA.

joined former First Lady "Lady Bird" Johnson for lunch. After a pleasant, relaxing lunch, we departed for Atlanta in a plane sent by President Carter—which took off from the runway built in the back of the Johnson house!

We learned that President Johnson himself had overseen construction of the runway during his presidency. The runway at the home is definitely a kind of extravagance I'm not familiar with, but I found it fascinating and enjoyable nonetheless.

Our research, along with the gracious assistance and kindness of President Carter, all came to fruition when the Martin Luther King, Jr., National Historic District was established.

For the sake of the historical record, there are a few facts I must add with respect to the King Center. The company responsible for the Center's construction was Holder Construction of Atlanta, Georgia, who, by the way, retained Isaac, my husband, as construction manager for the project. Herman Russell Construction Company worked along with Holder.

The architect was J. Max Bond of New York, whose inspiration for the reflecting pool surrounding ML's crypt was the beautiful pool of water leading to India's magnificent Taj Mahal.

21

FOUNDING THE MARTIN LUTHER KING, JR., CHILD DEVELOPMENT CENTER

*B*efore his death, ML had conceived the idea of developing an urban oasis that would include low-rent garden apartments and a high-rise housing facility. The complex would also include a downtown supermarket, business offices, and quality childcare for low-income families. The Southern Christian Leadership Conference (SCLC) would relocate its offices from Auburn Avenue to this development. The entire project was to be funded by a program sponsored by the United States Department of Housing and Urban Development (HUD).

After ML's death, the garden apartments and the high-rise facility were completed. However, the complete vision would not be realized. Much of the momentum was lost, as were the plans to construct a supermarket and have the SCLC relocate to that project site.

Despite these setbacks, I believed we should move forward with the childcare component and complete the work ML had envisioned. As usual, the challenge was money and funding. We wrote grant proposals. We sought corporate funding. Daddy pitched in to help with fund-raising. From the state of Georgia, with the assistance of Representative Georgiana Sinkfield, and from a variety of other sources, we were able to secure the resources required to open the doors of the Child Development Center.

We hired a full-time staff, which included a director, and faculty. Drucilla Tuggle was our first director. Sherri Jordan succeeded her, and I am proud to say the center's last director was my son, Isaac Jr., who now serves as president and CEO of the Martin Luther King, Jr., Center for Nonviolent Social Change.

Our board of directors consisted of Ms. Rita Samuels of the National Coalition of Black Women, Ms. Betty Dixon, Elise Gilham, Worth Chrisler, my old friend Dr. Dolores Robinson, Dr. Evelyn Chisholm, Representative Sinkfield, and Brunetta Lucas Bolton.

We leased our initial space for the center, as I said, from the Atlanta Housing Authority. Recently however, the authority struck a deal with the federal government pursuant to which low-income apartments were razed and replaced with mixed-use developments consisting of housing, some of it subsidized, together with office and retail space.

Alas, gentrification had reached Atlanta's Old Fourth Ward.

A few years ago, with great sadness and regret, we decided to close the Martin Luther King, Jr., Child Development Center.

22

EBENEZER BAPTIST CHURCH:
MY SPIRITUAL ROCK

*R*eferred to by many as one of the world's most famous freedom churches, Ebenezer Baptist Church has been an intimate part of the lives of the King family, and I am the granddaughter, daughter, and sister of ministers of this wonderful institution. Ebenezer is in my blood. My life has been entwined with this church—from the moment I was born.

I took my first breath one block from its front door; I was active in its youth groups and sang in its choirs. I attended its services and we conducted the funerals of both my parents and both my brothers there. I was married there and attended countless other weddings and funerals there, I went to its Sunday school.

The day I joined Ebenezer, there was a guest minister leading a revival. I walked down the aisle and stood there in front of the congregation acknowledging my desire to be baptized. No sooner had I had reached the front of the sanctuary than ML made his way down the aisle and joined me. He was quoted years later as saying, "After seeing her join I decided that I would not let her get ahead of me." His competitive streak surfaced early.

While I experienced many tragic, sad, heartbreaking moments at Ebenezer, I've had many more moments of joy there—for instance, my participation in the youth choir when I was a child. Those Sundays when we sang were special.

Normally, I sat in the pews with my family like everyone else. But on the days the youth choir performed, I got the special treat of sitting at the front of the church and looking out over the congregation during the service. Now, think about this from a young girl's perspective. I got to see who came in late, which of my friends got in trouble for talking during the service, who was spanked for chewing gum, who fell asleep—and who was wearing what. Being seated with the choir indeed offered a great perspective for a kid.

Often after morning services, we'd stroll down the street to the corner of Auburn Avenue and Butler Street to the famed Yates and Milton Drugstore.

The historians will tell you that Yates and Milton was one of the cornerstone black businesses on Auburn Avenue during its heyday. But I'd tell you that its claim to fame was the soda fountain, and the best hot dogs in town. I should note here that Butler Street is now named Jesse Hill Drive, in honor of the pioneering African American businessman who for years was president of the Atlanta Life Insurance Company. He has been a longtime supporter of our family, a patron of the civil rights movement, and a former chairman of the board of the King Center.

After our interludes at Yates and Milton, we'd return home for Sunday dinner. The spread on the table, as I've mentioned previously, would often include collard greens, macaroni and cheese, cabbage, baked chicken and dressing, candied yams, cakes, pies, peach cobbler with crusts that melted in my mouth like butter, and pretty much anything else imaginable.

Following these feasts, we'd fight the urge to pass out from satisfaction and return to Ebenezer for meetings of the Baptist Training Union (BTU). During my adolescence, the BTU was headed by Mrs. Nanniene Crawford, whom I have referred to previously. In addition to being a longtime family friend, Mrs. Crawford was a gifted and wonderful cook. She baked cakes that can only be described as out of this world.

After BTU came Sunday evening services.

Also with great fondness I recall when ML delivered his trial sermon at Ebenezer in 1947. He was an eighteen-year-old junior at Morehouse. I can picture Daddy now, sitting stone-faced, trying unsuccessfully to contain his visible, fatherly pride as his oldest son delivered his first sermon and took his first steps toward a career in the ministry. The sermon started out in the church basement, but eventually had to be moved upstairs to the main sanctuary to accommodate the overflowing crowd.

The congregation hung on every word ML uttered. When he finished, the audience rushed to the pulpit to congratulate him and shake his hand. And there, to the side, stood our proud and beaming father—finally able to flash the broad grin he'd been trying so hard all evening to suppress.

We all knew he was on his way to a life in the ministry. What we had no way of knowing was just how much he, Ebenezer, and the world would be changed as a result.

All those world-altering events evolved directly from the foundation of our faith and our broadly inclusive worldview of justice, peace, and equality, which were instilled in him from our earliest days in that red brick church on Atlanta's Auburn Avenue.

As an adult, long after my "career" with the youth choir came to an end, I remained involved with music at Ebenezer. Under the auspices of the Courtesy Guild, I gave a recital as a soprano soloist.

The guild had been organized by ML, and Coretta served as its chair. Mrs. Ada Slocum and Mrs. Eunice Simmons were its cochairs. Mrs. Marjorie Mc-Cray served as secretary, assisted by Mrs. Jimmie Thomas. Mrs. Slocum pulled double duty, also serving as the guild's financial secretary. Mrs. Ruth Davis served as chaplain, assisted by Mrs. Bernice Roberts.

THIS PHOTO WAS TAKEN AT MY RECITAL AT EBENEZER.

I have humorous and particularly fond memories of the recital. It was held on the occasion of the guild's sixth anniversary. The evening was exciting and, naturally, somewhat tense for me. I wouldn't say I was nervous—let's just say I had a touch of the butterflies that have been known to accompany public performances.

After the prelude and special organ music were presented by Mrs. Xernona B. Clayton, Mrs. Ruth Green led us in prayer. The program opened with Handel's "Thanks be to Thee"; I also sang Strauss's "My Hero (The Chocolate Soldier)," and the finale was Price's "My Soul's Been Anchored in the Lord."

The humor came in when, at some point during the evening, my daughter, Angela, who was then quite young, spied me and erupted into gleeful shouts of "Mama!! . . . Mama!!!!!"

The other experience was even funnier. Isaac Jr. had been assigned the task of coming to the stage and delivering me a gift of flowers after the performance. He walked briskly toward me. I was expecting a kiss or congratulations from my son, but he simply couldn't contain himself. He was dying to tell me that his cousin Martin III, as he said, "took my bubblegum."

It was priceless.

In terms of the church's involvement in the community, I also can't forget Ebenezer's pioneering foray into the broadcast arena. AD was the driving force behind a television series we had for a number of years on WAGA-TV 5. This was his brainchild. He did all the organizing and preliminary work in bringing it to life. But he eventually convinced me to get involved and to ultimately head the project.

The show aired Sunday mornings at nine o'clock. We taped it earlier in the week, on Wednesday evenings, at the studios of Channel 5. After a number of years, we changed, and began to tape the shows right on location at Ebenezer. The shows were timely and insightful, and we addressed a number of the current issues of the day. We had an impressive run of, I'd say, ten years or so before our current broadcast began.

Throughout its existence, Ebenezer has been known for innovative and cutting-edge programs. In addition to our pioneering, early involvement in religious broadcasting, sometime around 1969, AD served as copastor and founded the Ebenezer Children's Chapel. The Children's Chapel was a program dedicated to the spiritual enrichment, biblical education, and oratorical training of young people aged five to twelve.

We have been committed since Ebenezer's inception to doing the work that we deem to be our Christian duty, in the immediate community, and out beyond—in the greater world.

In so doing, we have always sought to feed the hungry, to clothe the poor, and to assist the downtrodden, whether that involved securing medical care, providing housing assistance, or any of the myriad other ministries and services we have assumed responsibility for furnishing,

As a body, Ebenezer's members have always taken this calling personally. ML reminded us over and over again, "Jesus has made it clear that he who is greatest among you shall be your servant."

I think it is also fair to say that Ebenezer's members believe that simply expressing compassion for the hardships and struggles faced by others is insufficient. Compassion must be coupled with action. Without some component of direct action, or intervention, compassion by itself is at worst meaningless to the person in need, and at best, it is simply unfulfilling in terms of serving the person's real needs.

Ebenezer's history is both intriguing and glorious. The church was founded in 1886, a mere nine years after the end of Reconstruction. A handful of parishioners started the institution, which was then located on Airline Street. It remained in that location, under Reverend John A. Parker's leadership, from 1886 to 1894. Reverend Parker, a man who had himself been born into slavery, was certainly the right man to guide the fledgling church during those tenuous times.

One of the unique facts that cause Ebenezer to be so exceptional is the small number of senior pastors who have served at its helm. In the entire 122 years of its existence, we have had only five senior pastors.

As I noted previously, my grandfather A. D. Williams was the second senior pastor to lead Ebenezer. His thirty-seven-year tenure lasted from March 14, 1894, until March 21, 1931—the day he passed away on his bedroom floor.

In addition to leading his flock in the church, Granddaddy Willims was extremely active in community, civic, and religious organizations. In 1904, he was elected president of the Atlanta Chapter of the Baptist Ministers Union. One of his proudest accomplishments, as he watched the membership grow by leaps and bounds, was to purchase land downtown on McGruder Street. He was so successful in increasing the membership that we eventually outgrew the McGruder Street location. As a result, Granddaddy led the congregation's move to a storefront located at 444 Edgewood Avenue.

In January 1913, Ebenezer's members purchased a plot of land at the corner of Jackson Street and Auburn Avenue. Shortly thereafter, a fund-raising campaign with a goal of twenty-five thousand dollars was announced. The following year, 1914, ground for the new structure was broken. Finally, eight long, hard years later, the proud new Ebenezer Baptist Church building rose along Auburn Avenue.

Daddy was our third and longest-serving senior minister. He served Ebenezer for a mind-boggling forty-four years. He was officially installed in October 1931, in the midst of the Depression. He retired on August 1, 1975.

As Ebenezer continued to grow, Dad increased his involvement on the national and international levels. When I was not quite seven years old, he traveled with a delegation of ministers from all across the United States to the Baptist World Alliance meeting in Berlin, Germany. While he was in Berlin, with peace-loving Christians from across the globe, Daddy saw the posters of Adolf Hitler plastered all about town and heard his menacing voice roar from sidewalk radios. While he didn't understand the German language, he intuitively knew the sound of the vile, evil, racist hatred coming from the man whom the world waited far too long to stop.

From July 14 through August 10, 1934, Daddy traveled by ship to France; then by train to Italy, and from Italy on to Africa, where he visited Tunisia, Libya, and Egypt.

While on the Egyptian leg of the trip, he went to Palestine and to the Holy Land.

Seeing Jerusalem, where Jesus lived and taught, proved to be especially moving and spiritually nourishing for him.

While Dad was traveling through Hitler's Germany, Hitler's cohort Benito Mussolini was preparing to wreak havoc in Ethiopia. The next year, in 1935, Mussolini invaded Ethiopia. In 1936, Ethiopia's proud leader, Emperor Haile Selassie, would be sent into exile. More than thirty years later, the emperor would be one of the first international guests to visit us following ML's death.

I had always been fascinated by the historical lineage of the emperor, which he traced directly to King Solomon and the Queen of Sheba. Moreover, I identified with his personal suffering, which had been great. During the Italian occupation, his daughter and grandchildren had been taken prisoner. Two of his sons-in-law were executed by the Italian army.

When the emperor visited us, it was so soon after ML's assassination that he was still entombed in his original resting place at Southview Cemetery. Because of his express desire to visit ML's tomb, we had a brief ceremony receiving the emperor at Southview. I greeted him there. He was fluent in French, and that's what we spoke during his visit. He was quite warm and charming. He expressed his delight at meeting "the sister of such a great and honorable man as Dr. King." For me, it was a truly humbling experience. He didn't spend a lot of time talking, but he did walk around the mausoleum quite a bit.

After the ceremony at Southview was over, the emperor went to Morehouse College, where he was awarded an honorary degree.

Ebenezer has hosted its fair share of dignitaries and world changers.

One of the earliest was Dr. Mary McCloud Bethune, who came to speak in January 1946. At the time, she was president of Daytona Beach's Bethune-Cookman College, which she had helped to found in 1904. She also served for years as the president of the National Conference of Negro Women.

Because of Mrs. Bethune's extraordinary friendship with Mrs. Eleanor Roosevelt, she was granted unprecedented access to the Roosevelt White House. She was, no doubt, the most influential black woman of her era.

Following Dad's retirement, Reverend Dr. Joseph Roberts, Jr., became Ebenezer's fourth senior pastor. He served from September 1975 to October 2005.

Dr. Roberts is a man of superior intellect, and he possesses gifts of deep compassion and spiritual conviction. His route to the leadership of Ebenezer is an interesting story.

Daddy recommended Dr. Roberts to the annual church conference in November 1974. The membership approved this recommendation.

Dad had been introduced to Reverend Roberts by a mutual friend, the Reverend William H. Gray III of Philadelphia. Gray pastored the Bright Hope Baptist Church and served several terms in the U.S. House of Representatives. After leaving Congress, Reverend Gray served as president of the United Negro College Fund.

There was as an impediment to Dr. Roberts's accepting the position at Ebenezer. At the time the offer was made, he was a director of the Presbyterian Church, U.S., and had been raised in the African Methodist Episcopal Church, where his father was a minister.

In order to lead Ebenezer, Dr. Roberts would have to change his church affiliation. He gladly did so. As a result, Reverend Joseph Roberts joined Ebenezer on January 5, 1975, and was baptized by Daddy. He began his tenure as our new minister.

Over the course of our existence, three copastors have served Ebenezer. Two of them were named King—ML (1960–68), AD (1968–69)—and the third was Reverend Dr. Otis Moss, Jr.

Our current senior pastor is a bright young Morehouse graduate, the Reverend Dr. Raphael Gamaliel Warnock. He has set about leading us on a course that addresses the needs of "the least of these" in the new millennium. Dr. Warnock's ministry addresses issues of the drug culture, poverty, HIV/AIDS, fair elections, the struggle to break the high school to prison pipeline that ensnares so many young black men, the pop culture's disrespect of women, and all the other social challenges of our day.

It is, after all, the Ebenezer Way!

ETERNALLY GRATEFUL AND MOVING
FORWARD—GOING STRONG

There has been a certain "duality" that characterizes my life experiences. Over the course of my eighty years, I have had many extraordinary experiences that have brought unimaginable joy and, at the opposite extreme, pain and grief.

My upbringing was that of a normal, middle-class African American family. But we were called upon, according to a supreme master plan, to perform extraordinary feats. My family was steeped in the fight for freedom and activism and that to us was normal. It was neither exceptional nor unusual to me. It's just the way things were.

Our roots in protest and advocacy for what is right run deep. My grandfather A. D. Williams, for example, worked closely with W. E. B. DuBois, the acclaimed intellectual, author, and activist. In 1906, Granddad, DuBois, and others formed the Georgia Equal Rights League to protest, among other things, the original incarnation of domestic terrorism, the lynch mob; the lease system for state prisoners; disparate treatment for blacks in the judicial system; the exclusion of black *men* from the voting rolls and juries; and inadequate and inferior segregated public schools.

My point is that whatever role my siblings, my parents, or I played in the civil rights movement, it came to us naturally. We saw it as simply doing God's will. I have always believed that the marches, the boycotts, and the direct-action tactics were all the very logical extension of what we learned was our duty as Christians. We saw our elders do it, we saw our parents do it, we saw our Ebenezer Church family do it, and we saw our larger community do it.

This is the lens through which most people view me. And rightly so, for it is the only glimpse they've been able to garner through the media and through viewing our private lives from afar. But AD, ML, and I were typical, active, outgoing children. We got into our fair share of trouble, we played pranks, we dated, we danced—not necessarily in accord with Daddy's wishes. We fell in love, married, and started families.

I like to believe that I am a well-rounded person. While circumstance and destiny have in some instances imposed tremendous responsibility on me, it has not always been as suffocating, serious, and as stifling as I believe the general perception would suggest.

The truth be told, I have a good sense of humor. I'm close to and cherish friends from childhood. I love my job and the forty-nine years I have been associated with Spelman College. I am now beginning my fiftieth year. I love to shop, to spend time with my family, and, whenever I have a moment to relax, it's a pretty safe bet you'll find me with a book in my hands.

And then there are the hats. Aside from my doll collection, if I have any *one* vice, it has to be the hats, I simply love them. I love shopping for and wearing them, whatever the occasion. A friend,

THIS PHOTO SHOWS MY WONDERFUL IMMEDIATE FAMILY: I'M JOINED AT MY EIGHTIETH BIRTHDAY CELEBRATION BY MY HUSBAND, ISAAC, DAUGHTER ANGELA, GRANDDAUGHTER, FARRIS CHRISTINE, AND SON ISAAC JR.

Herman "Skip" Mason, Morehouse's college archivist and associate dean, once introduced me by claiming that people in Atlanta waited all year to see what type of hat I would be wearing, or "unveiling," at the annual commemorative service we hold at Ebenezer during the celebration of ML's birth.

I can't speak to whether anyone actually gives my hats any thought, but I *can* gladly confirm that I look forward to the event each year, and that I know I will have selected a *special* hat for the occasion.

Of all the things one could be enamored of in this world, I suppose my hat thing ain't so bad.

I must also freely admit that one of the by-products of living this extraordinary life has been that I have been afforded an opportunity to have some exceptional experiences, and I've been able to meet some incredible people along the way. Included among them have been a number of U.S. presidents.

For example, I attended a private Oval Office meeting with President Ronald Reagan on the day he signed the legislation establishing ML's birthday as a national holiday. In addition to the natural sense of pride I felt in my brother and his accomplishments, my chest also swelled with a goodly portion of motherly pride, as well.

Vice President George Bush had been assigned to escort our group, which included Coretta, ML's children, Isaac, and me, along with our children, into the meeting with President Reagan.

As Vice President Bush was introducing my son Isaac to the president, he went on and on about the remarks he had heard Isaac give as he introduced his grandfather at a tribute dinner in Atlanta that Mr. Bush had attended. He told the president how thoughtful and articulate Isaac's introduction of Daddy was, and how impressive he had been.

What mother would not be elated in that situation? After our brief chat with the president and vice president, we were led out to the Rose Garden where the official ceremonial signing of the birthday legislation took place.

Of course, President Reagan was well known for his sense of humor. The mere mention of Isaac and his oratory caused the president to light up and say to us, "You know . . . that reminds me of the story of an old preacher in Texas," as he launched into one of his patented jokes.

On another occasion, perhaps two years later, I returned to the White House for another program in connection with ML's birthday. This time, Coretta and I were joined by, among others, two of

ML's closest aides and most trusted advisors, Reverend Ralph David Abernathy and Reverend Hosea Williams.

I have already spoken about the closeness of our family with President and Mrs. Jimmy Carter. We spent a wonderful evening in the Carter White House on one occasion when the musical entertainment was provided by the Morehouse College Glee Club.

One year, President Bill Clinton joined us in Atlanta to speak at ML's commemorative birthday service at Ebenezer.

And finally, I've had the opportunity to meet President George W. Bush twice. The first time was when he traveled to Atlanta and laid a wreath at ML's tomb. The second occasion was when we traveled to the White House for the unveiling of a portrait of ML, which is now prominently displayed.

MY SON, ISAAC JR., AND ME WITH PRESIDENT BILL CLINTON AT A KING CENTER COMMEMORATIVE SERVICE.

That trip was especially memorable, because we set out for Washington directly from the Ebenezer commemorative service, aboard Coca-Cola's corporate jet. Our journey that day was arranged and coordinated by Ingrid Saunders Jones, senior vice president of the Coca-Cola Company and chairperson of the Coca-Cola Foundation, who has been a longtime supporter of the King Center, and of our family.

It's no secret that the one thing on earth that brings me my greatest pleasure is my family. I'm pleased to report that my children, Isaac Jr. and Angela, have blossomed into fine, wonderful, caring, sensitive adults. Angela, as I proudly noted earlier, has given Isaac and me a beautiful granddaughter, Farris, who is well on her path to becoming an attorney and started middle school last fall. Now, of course, in my way of looking at it, she has only six years before she sets foot on campus as a freshman member of the Spelman College Class of 2018.

Isaac Jr. makes us proud every day as he goes about the demanding tasks required of him as president and CEO of the Martin Luther King, Jr., Center for Nonviolent Social Change. As I have braggingly reported on these pages, I am blessed to report for work each morning at Spelman, where Angela, Dr. Angela Farris Watkins, Ph.D., is an associate professor of psychology.

There's no doubt in my mind that my brothers would join me in beaming with pride at the development of their children as well.

AD and Naomi were blessed with five children. I have recounted the unfortunate deaths of two of them, Esther Darlene and Alfred D. W. (AL) King III. Their surviving siblings are Derek, Alveda, and Vernon.

Reverend Derek B. King is assistant to the pastor of Ebenezer

Baptist Church of Indianapolis, Indiana. Derek has two sons, Kyle and Derek Jr. Alveda King, a former Georgia state representative, and minister herself, has five children—three boys, Jarrett Ellis, Eddie Clifford Beal III, and Joshua John, and two daughters, Darlene Ruth Celeste and Jennifer. AD's youngest child, Reverend Vernon King, is pastor of the First Baptist Church of Greensboro, North Carolina. He and his wife, Robin, have two daughters, Venus and Victoria.

ML, as the world knows, was the father of four children. I have recounted the tragic death of Yolanda, who will always be lovingly remembered by us as simply Yoki. Yoki's baby sister, Elder Bernice A. King of the New Birth Missionary Baptist Church of Atlanta, is a Spelman graduate and holds a law and theological degree from Emory University. ML's younger son, Dexter (named after the Dexter Avenue Baptist Church), lives in Malibu, California, where he manages the licensing, copyright, and intellectual property transactions of the estate of Martin Luther King, Jr. Finally, there is Martin Luther King III, a Morehouse graduate and former member of the Fulton County (Georgia) Commission. Martin is now chairman and CEO of Realizing the Dream, Inc., where he develops and pursues new strategies for confronting issues of health care, economic prosperity, education, crime, war, and democracy in the twenty-first century.

I have to take a moment to say that I personally feel a special sense of redemption and fulfillment in thinking back over ML's life and work. We have recently watched an intense Democratic presidential primary campaign, one in which we watched, with pride and satisfaction, as a woman and an African American man battled to become the standard-bearer for one of the nation's two major political parties, a contest for election to the most powerful office in the world.

I can only sit back in awe and with pride when I consider that on August 28, 2008—forty-five years *to the day* after ML told the nation about his dream for "equality, justice . . . a day where men would be judged by the content of their character and not by the color of their skin"— the Democratic Party nominated an African American, Senator Barack Obama, for president of the United States. I was there to witness the moment.

HERE I AM, PROUD OF MY PAST AND CONFIDENTLY FACING WHATEVER THE FUTURE MAY HOLD.

ML was right: The arc of the moral universe *is* long, but it *does* bend toward justice.

And finally, but certainly not least, it gives me immense pride and pleasure to note that Martin and his wife, Arndrea Waters King, in May 2008 welcomed ML and Coretta's first grandchild with the arrival of seven-pound-five-ounce Yolanda Renee King, proving once again, that we, the King family, continue to grow, continue to love, and are . . . *Still Standing, Still Moving, and Still Serving . . . Through It All.*

MRS. KING FARRIS AND SENATOR BARACK OBAMA IN THE SANC-
TUARY OF EBENEZER BAPTIST CHURCH, TAKEN JANUARY 20,
2008, THE DAY BEFORE MARTIN LUTHER KING JR. DAY. SENATOR
OBAMA VISITED EBENEZER TO WORSHIP AND OFFER A FEW RE-
MARKS ON MLK. "I'M PROUD TO STAND WITH A BLACK PRESIDEN-
TIAL CANDIDATE," SAID MRS. KING FARRIS.

ACKNOWLEDGMENTS

As I pondered about a title for this memoir, I was overwhelmed at the thought of finding a few words that would capture the story of my life. Eighty-one years is a long time and I have been through so much. It was my dear husband of forty-eight years, who knows my story almost as well as I do, who reminded me of a familiar church hymn, "Through It All." As he said these words, they resonated in my spirit. I could hear the lines, "Through it all. I've learned to trust in Jesus. I've learned to trust in God." Indeed, I am grateful to God for this gift of life, with all of its sweet and bittersweet moments. I am absolutely convinced that God's love and blessings have ordered my life. To God Be the Glory!

I also owe a debt of gratitude to my beloved mother, Alberta Williams King; my father, Martin Luther King, Sr.; my brothers, Martin Luther King, Jr. (ML) and Alfred Daniel Williams King (AD); my grandfather and grandmother, Reverend Adam Daniel Williams and Jennie Celeste Williams; and my aunt Ida Worthem. Though none of us realized that I would be the last one of our household on this side of life, history will show that God's infinite wisdom allowed each of them to pour into me an unshakable amount of strength and courage. At my core lies the spirit of each of them. I am filled with their immeasurable love. They are remarkable!

I am forever blessed by my husband, Isaac Sr. His shoulders have been strong enough to uphold me through all of my trials and his smiles have been wide enough to embellish all of my triumphs. I shall be eternally thankful for his love. My children, Isaac Jr. and Angela, are the joys of my life. They made a real Mama out of me. The pride I have for them has lifted me up over and over again. As they continue to make their own marks in life, they extend mine. My granddaughter, Farris Christine, is Grandma's "Puddin' Pie." She has added a heap of love to my heart. She amazes me! All of my work is done with an eye toward her future.

My extended family members, from the King and Farris sides, have encouraged me to write my story. Their support has helped me to realize the real importance of this for our family. Ours is a special bond. Each of them has a special place in my heart. I am also mindful of the part of my journey enriched by my sister-in-law Coretta (more like a sister to me) and all of my other departed loved ones. Their spirits continue to anchor me.

I bear in my heart the biggest trophy for my colleagues and students at Spelman College, both past and present. So much of what is written here has been born out of the forty-nine years of day-to-day interactions with them. Special thanks to the Spelman College presidents under whom I have worked; the late Dr. Albert E. Manley,

Dr. Donald M. Stewart, Dr. Johnetta Betsch Cole, Dr. Audrey Forbes Manley, and Dr. Beverly Daniel Tatum, our present leader.

My Ebenezer Baptist Church family has always been near and dear to me. Many thanks to my pastor, Reverend Dr. Raphael G. Warnock, my pastor emeritus, Reverend Dr. Joseph L. Roberts, Jr., and the entire Ebenezer family for their unwavering love and support. The name "Ebenezer" is symbolically represented in the Bible as a stone of help. For me, it has been true to its symbolism. "Here I raise mine Ebenezer. Hither By Thy Help I'm Come!"

The Martin Luther King, Jr., Center for Nonviolent Social Change, Inc. now the King Center, is an organization to which I have given my earnest and life-long commitment. I am proud of its sustaining power. I owe a very special thanks to the King Center staff, each of whom possesses a passion to share with the world the moral and ethical principles of my brother Martin. I am especially thankful for Barbara Harrison, Steve Klein, and Eric Tidwell. And all the King Center Staff.

I want to also acknowledge the tremendous support of a few individuals who aid me in my day-to-day travels, accompanying me on various trips out of the city and to many local events. Indeed, they are divinely assigned. They give of themselves, unselfishly, time and time again. They are Yvonne Hodge, Rachel Martin, Cass Miller, Dolores Robinson, Vernice Tuggle, Donald Richardson, Ozie J. Adams, and Blanche Thrash. Thanks also to Fuery Reid, Zeric Foster, and *Roger Babb* for their invaluable assistance with the preparation of this book.

My administrative assistant, Jacqueline Bass, has worked with me in the Learning Resources Center at Spelman College for twelve years. I appreciate her many contributions. She has enhanced my efficiency in extraordinary ways. Special thanks to my colleagues in the Learning Resources Center, Lula Roberts and Cynthia Hodges Atkins.

I salute my Washington High classmates of 1944 and my Spelman College classmates of 1948. I will always remember the significance of our school days. Without a doubt, we were ripened at the right places.

I also want to express a special thanks to my literary agent, Jennifer Lyons. Thanks also to my editor Malaika Adero and Krishan Trotman.

Special thanks to my dear sisters of Alpha Kappa Alpha Sorority, Inc., and the Buckhead Cascade Chapter of the Links, Inc. Our sisterly ties are unforgettable.

I am also appreciative of the many friends and neighbors of the Collier Heights Community. There is so much untold history in the soul of our community.

Finally, this memoir would not have been possible without the writing assistance of attorney Richard Grigsby. His talent is unmatched! I am grateful for his understanding, his patience, his brilliance, and his willingness to saturate his thoughts with the story of my life.

Thanks also to Vincent Tolliver for his assistance.

Thank You All!

INDEX

NOTE: Bold page numbers refer to picture captions. **CKF** refers to Christine King Farris; **MLK** refers to Martin Luther King, Jr.; **MLK Sr** refers to Martin Luther King, Sr.; **Mother Dear** refers to Alberta Christine Williams King.